The Sent, The Removed, and The Disqualified

BISHOP BART PIERCE

The Sent, The Removed, and The Disqualified

"And how shall they preach unless they are sent?"
—Romans 10:15

Strawbridge Press
1607 Cromwell Bridge Road
Baltimore, MD 21234

The Sent, The Removed, and The Disqualified

rockcitychurch.com

Cover Design by Daniel Epps

The Sent, The Removed, and The Disqualified only available at
rockcitychurch.com

The following abbreviations are used to identify other
versions of the Bible in this book:

Nouns and pronouns referring to Deity are capitalized
throughout the text unless they are included within a direct
quotation, in which case the original capitalization is retained.
Bold and italic in Scriptures were added by the Author.

ISBN: 979-8-218-21303-9

Strawbridge Press, 1607 Cromwell Bridge Road, Baltimore, MD 21234

rockcitychurch.com

Printed in the United States of America ▪ May 2023

Foreword

This book is an important training manual to help develop church leaders into effective Equippers. It is a tool for fivefold leaders who equip believers for the work of ministry. It will help churches to build an army, not an audience.

Bishop Pierce has a deep passion to see more church leaders rise to their responsibility to prepare and mobilize the people to do what God created them to do. He believes that now, more than ever, it is important for all church leaders to understand that winning people to Christ and providing a church home is not their primary role and function. Instead, it is equipping the saints for ministry. He also understands that it is not the leader's role to do all the work of ministry alone.

Christ has a mission for the church to spread the Gospel to all nations. As Bishop Pierce argues, the Great Commission (Matthew 28:19) cannot be accomplished by any one person or group of people. Rather, the whole church is needed to fulfill it, but they must be equipped so that this mandate can be achieved.

In Section 1, Bishop Pierce draws on his personal experiences as he discusses the church as a sending station, a principle that Jesus Himself modeled by commissioning the Apostles and others (Mark 3:14-15, 6:7; Luke 10:1-2; Matthew 28:18-20). This approach to ministry promotes multiplication rather than addition. It also prevents burn-out (Exodus 18:13-22), which unfortunately is too common among church leaders today.

In Section 2, Bishop Pierce describes the attributes and lifestyle of an effective Equipper and answers questions like these:

How do you equip the saints?

How do you become an effective Equipper?

Section 3 looks at the benefits and rewards of those who are being equipped.

Section 4 explains in more detail how leaders should accurately respond to the three groups of people they will encounter during the equipping process—the Sent, the Removed, and the Disqualified.

These chapters will encourage church leaders and deepen your understanding of and appreciation for the equipping process.

I believe that this book is highly important for fivefold leaders today. It is an invaluable resource and should be required reading for every Bible school or training program.

Every church leader must be knowledgeable about how to effectively equip believers to do what they were created to do and fulfill the mandate of Christ.

Apostle Dr. John A. Tetsola

Ecclesia Word Ministries International, President
Reformers Ministries International, Presiding Apostle and Founder

Endorsements

Having had the privilege of knowing Bishop Bart Pierce for over two decades, I consider it a tremendous honor to call him my spiritual father and covering. Not only is he an accomplished builder of physical structures such as churches and houses, but he is also a builder within the body of Christ. He is a leader among leaders, an equipper of the saints, and an influencer of influencers. There are many who may offer blessings, but only a select few have the ability to truly build you up. In his book, "The Sent, The Removed, and The Disqualified," Bishop Bart Pierce shares over forty years of experience, valuable nuggets of insights from the Holy Spirit, and a wealth of practical advice that can help leaders of all types and callings take their next steps forward.

Dr. Paul Tan
Apostle of City Blessing Churches Worldwide
President of World Blessing Foundation

The Sent, the Removed, and the Disqualified by Bishop Apostle Bart Pierce is a well-written exegete of scripture regarding the church as God's apostolic mission-sending center. At the same time, it is full of revelation and somewhat auto biographical because Bart Piece is a practitioner of everything written in this book. I highly recommend this book, especially to anyone in the ascension gifts ministry. Please read it with the leading of the Holy Spirit and receive the wisdom, knowledge, and revelations within these pages!

John P. Kelly
International Convenor of the International Coalition of Apostolic Leaders (ICAL)

Bishop Bart Pierce has done it again! Another great book that's simple yet so very profound that few people really get it, embrace it, and do it in their lives as ministry leaders. Our responsibility to empower both kings and priests for the expansion of the Kingdom of God in the earth must become our upmost priority. That's why this book is so important. We can no longer just do church services. The Church must become an equipping center to develop fivefold ministry gifts and to build marketplace leaders to make a difference and impact our culture.

Dr. Keith Johnson
Success Strategist

Bishop Pierce does it again! *The Sent, The Removed, and The Disqualified* is a "now" word for leaders, pastors, and fivefold ministers of our day. This book clearly lays out the importance of what it means to live and minister as "sent ones". God takes all leaders through a qualifying process in which He uses fivefold ministers to test, equip, and empower His people for the work of the ministry. We also see that those who try to bypass God's process are often removed or disqualified. This book will guide many leaders for years to come.

Jim Kilmartin,
Senior Pastor, Center City Church Altoona PA.

I have known Bishop Bart Pierce for almost three decades. His giftings, his experiences, and his accomplishments in Kingdom advancement are expansive. The experiences, underlying this manual are tested and proven. This manual is a response to Paul's encouragement to Timothy. "You should teach people whom you can trust the things you and many others have heard me say. Then they will be able to teach others." 2 Timothy 2:2 (NCV)

Bishop Joseph L. Garlington
Founding Pastor
Covenant Church of Pittsburgh

Presiding Bishop
Reconciliation Ministries International

Contents

SECTION 1. THE CHURCH IS A SENDING STATION

"And the Lord added to the church daily those who were being saved."—Acts 2:47

"Unless the LORD builds the house, They labor in vain who build it; Unless the LORD guards the city, The watchman stays awake in vain."—Psalm 127:1

"And this is eternal life, that they may know You, the only true God, and Jesus Christ whom You have sent."—John 17:3

"And Jesus came and spoke to them, saying, 'All authority has been given to Me in heaven and on earth. Go therefore and make disciples of all the nations, baptizing them in the name of the Father and of the Son and of the Holy Spirit, teaching them to observe all things that I have commanded you." —Matthew 28:18-20

"And the evil spirit answered and said, 'Jesus I know, and Paul I know; but who are you?'"—Acts 19:15

SECTION 2. EQUIPPING THE SAINTS

Section 3. What You Receive from An Anointed Equipper

"If I am not an apostle to others, yet doubtless I am to you. For you are the seal of my apostleship in the Lord."—1 Corinthians 9:2

". . . but be filled with the Spirit, speaking to one another in psalms and hymns and spiritual songs, singing and making melody in your heart to the Lord, giving thanks always for all things to God the Father in the name of our Lord Jesus Christ, submitting to one another in the fear of God."—Ephesians 5:18-21

"And if you have not been faithful in what is another man's, who will give you what is your own?" —Luke 16:12

"For Satan himself transforms himself into an angel of light. Therefore it is no great thing if his ministers also transform themselves into ministers of righteousness, whose end will be according to their works." —2 Corinthians 11:14-15

"But one and the same Spirit works all these things, distributing to each one individually as He wills." —1 Corinthians 12:11

"But the LORD said to Samuel, 'Do not look at his appearance or at his physical stature, because I have refused him. For the LORD does not see as man sees;

for man looks at the outward appearance, but the LORD looks at the heart.'"—1 Samuel 17:7

"But those who wait on the LORD Shall renew their strength; They shall mount up with wings like eagles, They shall run and not be weary, They shall walk and not faint."—Isaiah 40:31

SECTION 4. THOSE WHO ARE SENT, REMOVED, OR DISQUALIFIED

"I heard the voice of the Lord, saying: "'Whom shall I send, And who will go for Us?' "Then I said, 'Here am I! Send me.'"—Isaiah 6:8

"But Paul insisted that they should not take with them the one who had departed from them in Pamphylia, and had not gone with them to the work."—Acts 15:38

"But Peter said, 'Ananias, why has Satan filled your heart to lie to the Holy Spirit and keep back part of the price of the land for yourself? While it remained, was it not your own? And after it was sold, was it not in your own control? Why have you conceived this thing in your heart? You have not lied to men but to God.'" —Acts 5:3-4

"And the same one who descended is the one who ascended higher than all the heavens, so that he might fill the entire universe with himself."—Ephesians 4:10 NLT

Author's Introduction. The Church Is a Sending Station

"And how shall they preach unless they are sent?"
—Romans 10:15

A s of November 2023, I will have been preaching in Baltimore for 40 years. My wonderful journey started in 1972 in Virginia Beach, Virginia. Just like the movie "Jesus Revolution," I was one of those hippies who stumbled into church. In my case, it was Rock Church in Virginia Beach with Pastors John and Anne Gimenez. It was a young church, established about five years earlier by a bunch of Methodists who invited in a lot of long-haired, drug-infested hippies like me.

God was in that house in a big way! I didn't have a clue what a church was supposed to be like. but soon we were being transformed by God's Word through the Holy Spirit. As we grew by the hundreds and then the thousands, we began to hear the call of God to preach.

The church was actively evangelizing all the hippies and sinners who came in off the streets. We were hungry for God, but we needed to be discipled. We all went to the local Bible school and began to develop a hunger for God's Word! It wasn't long before we would be sent from this local church to start new churches. Over a hundred new churches sprang up along the East Coast, the Midwest, and then Africa and the islands of the sea.

I was given the assignment of going to those churches to help them solve problems that arose. Finally, in 1983, I was sent to start my own church in Baltimore, and I am still here. We started with a small group of about 15 people. Within five months, we had grown to 500. We built a new sanctuary. It was paid for when we moved in! Then we built a school for students K-5 through Grade 12. In seven years, we had grown to 2,000, so we built our next large sanctuary to hold 3,000 people. God has been good to us.

To date, I've planted more than 50 churches. In Madagascar, we have 30 churches. In Ghana, Africa, we have nine churches. We have churches in other parts of America and in Indonesia. And the movement is still growing.

In all these church plantings, I have learned that the key to success is those who are Sent. Romans 10:15 says, "And how shall they preach unless they are sent?" Jesus said that He was sent, and the disciples were sent.

To become a church planter, first you are Equipped, then you are Sent. It is an honor and a great responsibility. In starting a church, you become an Equipper. You continue the biblical pattern of equipping new shepherds and sending them out. Those Sent Ones build strong, healthy, local churches that multiply again and replenish the earth with the real Gospel of the Kingdom.

During the years that we have equipped and sent out saints to plant churches and ministries, some were Removed for a season, for their good and the good of God's work. However, they rejoined us later, in the right season. Then they were able to fulfill their purpose, making their calling and election sure.

Unfortunately, some never finished the race. They were the Disqualified. As hard as that is, it's often necessary.

In this book I have explained how to discern the differences among these three groups—the Sent, the Removed, and the Disqualified. When the church understands how these groups differ and how to manage them effectively, it will enable God's end-time church to multiply and make an impact. Then strong local churches can bring God's Kingdom to earth.

Let's do it right. We don't have to keep redoing it over again! Equippers, this is the manual you need so you can mature your church and turn cities upside down for Jesus!

Hungry for Him,

Bishop Bart Pierce
Senior Pastor, Rock City Church, Baltimore

Section 1.

The Church Is a Sending Station

1. How a Hippie Was Added to the Church

*"And the Lord added to the church daily those
who were being saved."—Acts 2:47*

When I was a hippie surfing off Virginia Beach in 1971, the last person I expected to meet was a Puerto Rican ex-con preacher from Spanish Harlem. I was like the other hippies of my generation before the Jesus Revolution. Drugs were a big part of my life—buying, selling, and using. I was a drug dealer on the run with a price on my head and a long string of arrests. I thought all church people were fakes.

Although I didn't know it at the time, John Gimenez, that preacher, had a shaky past, too. He was shooting drugs in New York until he walked into a storefront church and met Jesus in 1963. By the time I met him, he was transformed. He went to London with a Christian singing group of converted guys called The Addicts where he met Pat Robertson, founder of CBN and "The 700 Club." They became lifelong friends. Brother John and his wife Sister Anne founded Rock Church in Virginia Beach and constantly went to the oceanfront and the streets, looking for people like me to bring to Jesus.

After Brother John got me to go to the church, I walked in the door and a little man came up and hugged me. I didn't know what to do. My wife was afraid I would knock him out because I had said to her in the car on the way there, "If one of those creeps hugs me, I'll knock him out."

Instead, Jesus melted my heart. My heart had become hardened because my mom died when I was nine, then my dad dropped dead when I was 17. I was devastated, but I never cried. I just became a big troublemaker. But when I got to Rock Church and knelt down before my God, I cried like a baby.

When I got back in the car, I tossed out the dope and never took drugs again.

If you have seen the 2023 movie "Jesus Revolution" about Greg Laurie and Lonny Frisbee and the hippies who walked into Calvary Chapel in Costa Mesa, California, pastored by Chuck Smith, you can picture my friends and me. After I was saved, I brought in many other hippies, and they got saved. Even though they were in California and we were on the East Coast, we were also getting saved in droves and filling up Rock Church.

To their credit, the fivefold at Rock Church not only welcomed us. They also saw our potential. They equipped us with Bible training and discipled us so we could be sent to do the work of the ministry. It was an equipping and sending church. Many of them now pastor churches, as I do. We are all still friends.

I have pastored Rock City Church in Baltimore since John Gimenez sent me there with my wife Coralee in 1983.

Even today I can still talk to people on drugs, from the hole, the streets, and all kinds of mess and bring them to Jesus. I can say, "You're not dead! Come forth out of those graves! Take off those grave clothes! Give your life to Jesus and be born again!"

Equipping Strengthens the Church to Bring Us Together

The "Jesus Revolution" movie was not only about success stories. It also depicted problems that can arise when people are thrust into ministry too soon and not equipped to handle it. Sometimes they are Removed for a time of greater spiritual growth. Other times, unfortunately, they are Disqualified.

This book is about bringing us back to the place where we are not only winning people to Jesus and providing a church home but also equipping the saints for the work of ministry. The fivefold ministry leaders need to be Equippers for the Sent.

We live in a culture today that is downgrading the church, where people think faith is only about their individual identity, who they are and who they want to be. People are so into their own personality and wanting to be their "Best Me." However, we're all part of one body of Christ. Being in one accord comes from an intimate connection with one another, not only for our common salvation but also for our common assignment.

In Paul's letters to the Ephesians and Corinthians he talks about how we're the hand and knee and elbow and we're all the parts of the same body. Every part has its function, but we're all part of the body. That's why the only group that can ever bring reconciliation of different races and different groups together is the church. The church's structure was designed so that when Jesus died, he did not die for any one ethnic group, He died for the world. If there's ever going to be unity, if there's ever going to be any kind of coming together as a people, it should be the church.

Unity Happens When You Equip God's People

We have every different nationality at my church, but we've become one. Unity happens when you equip God's people. It's powerful. You don't have people just dragging along, coming along for all the wrong reasons. When you have equipping going on, everybody's here because of Jesus. Everybody is here because they want more of Him. Everybody is here to worship Him.

We can even see the difference between a Thursday night service and a Sunday service. On Sundays you've got this eclectic group of all kinds of people, and you don't necessarily have the same harmony, the same sense of oneness that you have on a Thursday night. The ones that come on Thursday night usually come because they are hungry for God and want something more.

Scriptures Unify More Than Social Issues

Everybody should know the doctrines of God. I say all the time that you should read your Bible. You should uphold the standard of Scripture. Your strongest stand won't be whether you believe or don't believe in abortion. It will be what you did with Christ and the revelation of who He is and the doctrines of God.

Baltimore, the Murder Capital of America, Needs Prayer

In 2022, Baltimore was the murder capital of America with the most murders per capita of any city in the United States.[1] On Resurrection Sunday 2023, our pastors' group Peace for the City held a sunrise prayer service at Baltimore's Inner Harbor.

Cities need pastors who pray together—men and women of strong character and sound doctrine and an active fivefold ministry that equips and sends leaders. Those who are Sent start more churches and ministries and unify with pastors until cities are transformed.

You violate Scripture when you claim a false remedy. You have to keep your mind on the Lord. That's how I got off drugs and started doing crazy things for the Lord, because I put my mind in His Book. I don't know anything else but the Bible. When you ask me questions, I'm going to give you this Word. My mind was renewed by the washing of the Word (*Ephesians 5:25*). If you have a city problem, you're not washing your mind with God's Word. You washed your feet, you washed your ears, but not your mind.

---

[1] Rushaad Hayward, "Study: Baltimore ranked as a top city with increase in homicide rates." Online at https://www.wmar2news.com/news/local-news/study-baltimore-ranked-as-a-top-city-with-increase-in-homicide-rates. Accessed April 2023.

The Body of Christ in a city represents many backgrounds and denominations, but we flow into one big mass of water—the kingdom of God. We want to be sure that those streams make glad the city of God (*Psalm 46:4*). That is why I am giving you here Bible-based success strategies to equip and send ministers to change cities through Christ and the church.

When Jesus stood in the bow of the boat, He said to the storm, "Peace! Be still!" He's in our boat today. We speak peace and declare peace over every disruption in our world. We will not give in to Satan and the works of evil. Our God is well able to do above all that we could ask or think. In the name of Jesus. Amen.

2. When the Sent Ones Guard the City

"Unless the LORD builds the house,
They labor in vain who build it;
Unless the LORD guards the city,
The watchman stays awake in vain."—Psalm 127:1

Several years ago, I went to Philadelphia to speak at a large conference for pastors and leaders. Brunch was provided for about 20 of the speakers and I was scheduled to share a few words with this small group before the main meeting.

While at the reception, I saw a pastor whom I had never met but whom I knew pastored the largest church in Philadelphia at the time, about 10,000 people. I went up to him and said, "Hi, my name is Bart Pierce. You know my pastor, John Gimenez."

He put down his plate and said, "John Gimenez! Oh my God, I love Johnny!" In those days, anybody who knew my pastor called him Johnny. He said, "I love him! You're his son?"

I said, "Yeah, I'm here today to speak on his behalf." That instantly opened a relationship. When I got to my table, I asked the guy to my left, "Excuse me. Would you mind trading seats with that gentleman over there? I'd like to have him sit beside me."

He said, "No problem," and the older man came up.

Before I addressed this group, the Lord showed me something about them, so I began with a question: "How many of you once knew this man as your pastor, but you left his church?"

The room froze.

Finally, one guy raised his hand. He started crying as he admitted, "I left." Then they all started weeping.

I looked over at the older gentleman and he was a mess. He had buried his face in his napkin. He was just bawling. I said to the audience, "Listen to me. I cannot go into that meeting of 2500 people and talk to them about how we need to come together in Philadelphia if you don't get this settled right here, right now."

The whole meeting began repenting and apologizing to the elder pastor. He was so gracious that he forgave everyone. He kept saying to different ones who came up to him, "No problem. I love you. I've been praying for you. I'm so glad to see you."

I knew God was going to heal them. I also knew I would probably have to do this again, because so many pastors leave the wrong way to start a ministry. *They were not sent. They just went.*

We Have Forgotten That We Are a Family

A church is like a marriage. The Bible says that Christ "loved the church and gave Himself for her" (Ephesians 5:25). Jesus loves the church, and He wants us to love one another as He loved us (John 13:34).

Pastors like the one I just mentioned get disappointed when people whom they believe love Jesus with all their hearts challenge their authority and expect to be served instead of serving. Sometimes they leave, and they don't leave well. Some even quit God. This road we're on ain't wide. It's narrow.

God's Focus Is the Sent, So Make Them *Your* Focus

The Father sent Jesus.

Jesus sent His disciples.

The church sent the apostles. Everyone was being sent.

- The Sent—Those you can successfully train and send
- The Removed—Those you set aside for more growth
- The Disqualified—Those you eliminate from consideration

Those Who Send Out Ministers Are the Fivefold

"And He Himself gave some to be apostles, some prophets, some evangelists, and some pastors and teachers, for the equipping of the saints for the work of ministry, for the edifying of the body of Christ."—Ephesians 4:11-12

Equipping the saints for the work of ministry in every generation is the work of the fivefold ministry in the church. These senior leaders should be continually equipping Christians with knowledge of the Bible, discipling them in the fruit of Christlike character, training them for spiritual warfare, then sending them to do the work of ministry. When those who are Sent run into problems, they know they can call on the leaders who raised them.

The Lord Guards the City When Its Pastors Were Sent

"And how shall they preach unless they are sent? As it is written: 'How beautiful are the feet of those who preach the gospel of peace, Who bring glad tidings of good things!'"—Romans 10:15

Those who are Sent is the emphasis of Romans 10:15. "And how shall they preach *unless they are sent?*"

Every city needs Sent Ones in the pulpits of its churches. Otherwise, the city is unguarded, and evil can flourish, which is the situation we see now.

"Unless the LORD builds the house,
They labor in vain who build it;
Unless the LORD guards the city,
The watchman stays awake in vain."—Psalm 127:1

Many pastors are godly and a credit to their community, but not everyone who operates a church or ministry has been Sent. Some send themselves. Some left a former church the wrong way, after rebelling against the pastor, and carry a seed of rebellion. Some are rebels against the Bible. Some dislike church structure.

Other ways that churches get built without the Lord are lack of knowledge of the Word, ignorance of the biblical definition of a church, and missing members of fivefold Equippers (Ephesians 4:11).

The Sent, the Removed, the Disqualified. Not everyone has the same anointing. This book equips the fivefold to identify and train the real candidates whom God has chosen to be Sent and not be distracted by those who should be Removed or Disqualified. It also warns the church to elevate people into ministry based on Christlike character and not the need for their skill to fill positions.

Every Church Must Build an Army, Not an Audience

If your church caters to an audience, those masses will quit and walk away, but if you train them like an army, they can be sent to change the world.

> *"Then the seventy returned with joy, saying, 'Lord, even the demons are subject to us in Your name.'"*
> *—Luke 10:17*

Churches That Have Bible Schools Are Unified by Faith

Bishop Joseph Mattera tells me that Rock City Church is one of the few churches in America that has a Bible School. No wonder no one guards the cities when there are preachers who have no business being in a pulpit. They were never trained in the Word or discipled in Christlike character. They are novices initiating their own ministries with their own faulty interpretations.

When preachers ask me why we have a Bible School in our church, I say the best times we have together are when everybody's in love with Jesus and knows Him as the Son of God.

> *"Till we all come to the unity of the faith, and of the knowledge of the Son of God, to a perfect man, to the measure of the stature of the fullness of Christ."* —Ephesians 4:13

When we all agree on Jesus and read His Book, we share the same faith that brings us into one accord. We have the same faith in the same God. The right spirit toward one another. It is something worth multiplying.

When church novices fail, their people don't know what to do. They float all over the place because they were put in front of a novice and the novice got puffed up. He destroyed what God intended that every true church should do.

A healthy church recreates itself in each new generation of leaders. It stands guard over the city, represents Jesus, equips and sends leaders who fill the earth with Christ.

Sent Ones Are Willing to Sacrifice for Jesus' Call

"So likewise, whoever of you does not forsake all that he has cannot be My disciple."—Luke 14:33

Today's feel-good, all-about-me, weekly entertainment churches are the opposite of Jesus' call. He said to count the cost. He sent disciples to preach the Gospel to every nation, knowing it could cost them their lives.

His disciples knew going out the door that they must be ready to die, as Jesus died, even if it were only death to self. They knew persecution was coming. They saw Stephen stoned to death.

The church has moved so far away from equipping people to die that we can't even get them to church on Sunday.

We need to know the Scriptures and be strong in these tough days.

Spiritual fathers help you grow up. With all that's going on in the church and in the world, we need a revival of fathering among church leaders. We need new leaders who understand tough love. They don't compromise on biblical standards for church members or themselves and have hearts of love.

Spiritual fathering is the primary church structure where the equipping of leaders should take place.

Not many mighty, not many noble, but sold-out saints becoming equipped in churches. That will transform cities.

> *"For we do not wrestle against flesh and blood, but against principalities, against powers, against the rulers of the darkness of this age, against spiritual hosts of wickedness in the heavenly places."*—Ephesians 6:12

Staying accountable to a spiritual father is a force of stability in personal growth and the growth of churches. When you are a son, then you learn to be a father to the next generation.

Masses Leave You but Disciples Reproduce You

After Jesus fed the 5,000, where did the masses go? They went home! People quit all the time and leave the things of God. The Bible says in the last days even the very elect will be fooled.

> *"For false christs and false prophets will rise and show great signs and wonders to deceive, if possible, even the elect."*—Matthew 24:24

But when pastors equip disciples, as Jesus did, the disciples become the Sent. They are committed. They want the Word. They want to be equipped for ministry. They do the work.

Some of today's members quit their churches as easily as they quit their marriages. They have a lousy, selfish attitude, and it's all about you. They get their little self-up on top of their shoulders and run away to do their own thing at another church or another marriage, even though Jesus never gave us a quick escape clause from either marriage or the church.

Just because a few things go wrong in marriage or the church, you don't disrespect your spouse or your pastor and leave the church or your family behind. We have a destiny together to do God's will and change our cities and the nations.

Many People Who Attend Church Don't Know the Basics

We have people sitting in church today who are not aware of the simplest things. They don't even know that Jesus rose from the dead. They are sitting there because they have always been sitting there or their parents took them or somebody invited them or all kinds of other reasons. They are not there to be trained and equipped and sent out to serve Jesus Christ in ministry.

One of the Basics—Mankind's Condition Is Called Sin

The Bible is written about a condition of mankind called sin and it's written about a Redeemer from sin, Jesus Christ. Jesus is the Lamb who was slain from the foundation of the world. He came to save and redeem fallen man. He didn't care what color the man was. He didn't care what size he was. He didn't care what kind of sin he had. Small sin, bad sin, white lie, black lie—it didn't matter. He was coming to save mankind!

> *"Repent therefore and be converted, that your sins may be blotted out, so that times of refreshing may come from the presence of the Lord."—Acts 3:19*

The church has turned the redemption that Jesus paid for with His blood into automatic forgiveness. People think, "I can live anyway I want. Whatever I do it's on *you* to forgive *me* if *you're* going to stay right with God." That's not true. Get right with God yourself. Repent of your own sins to God. You have offended God. Let God deal with the other person Himself.

Jesus Died Once for All

Under the old covenant, priests offered daily sacrifices for sin—their own sins and the sins of the nation. But Jesus died once for all. He became God's guarantee of a better covenant.

> *"Jesus has become a surety of a better covenant."*
> *—Hebrews 7:22*

Jesus took all the sin of all the world upon Himself. He took it and He died for that sin, as Hebrews 7 says, once for all.

> *". . . who does not need daily, as those high priests, to offer up sacrifices, first for His own sins and then for the people's, for this He did once for all when He offered up Himself."—Hebrews 7:27 .*

Your Salvation Comes *After* You Repent

Salvation doesn't just happen because God says, "OK. I'm going to save you." Then the switch goes on and you're ecstatic. You weren't even looking for that? You didn't even want Jesus?

No. Come to the altar yourself. Repent and say, "I'm a sinner. I am sorry. Please forgive me."

I'm telling every young man and woman whom I run into, every young leader, to not only get saved but also get ahold of God. Get ahold of the Word. Study! Get some training.

If you desire ministry, you need to be in Bible school. You need to get in front of the Word. You need to get in front of prophets. You need to get ahold of the plan of God for you, because if we're going to equip you, we have to equip you for the purpose of ministry. God can't use you unless you know the truth. If you desire ministry at all, you better get busy doing some serious studying, because if you're not studying now there is no way that God can use you.

When an intellectual demonic force sweeps through the church, pontificating great things that swell up out of its imagination, your best defense is the truth. You must know the truth. You must be able to define the truth and preach the truth.

> *Jesus said, "And you shall know the truth, and the truth shall make you free."—John 8:32*

3. Jesus Was Sent

"And this is eternal life, that they may know You, the only true God, and Jesus Christ <u>whom You have sent</u>."—John 17:1-3

Jesus knew the Father sent Him. He said, in essence, "I'm His Son. He sent Me. I'm doing what He sent me to do. I'm saying what He sent Me to say. I carry His glory. I carry His perfection. I maintain His standards. I bring people into one accord, just like My Father."

> *"And I know that His command is everlasting life. Therefore, whatever I speak, **just as the Father has told Me**, so I speak."—John 12:50*

> *"I do not pray for these alone, but also for those who will believe in Me through their word; that they all may be one, as You, Father, are in Me, and I in You; that they also may be one in Us, **that the world may believe that You sent Me.**"—John 17:20-21*

> *"Father, I desire that they also whom You gave Me may be with Me where I am, that they may behold My glory which You have given Me; for You loved Me before the foundation of the world. O righteous Father! The world has not known You, but I have known You; and **these have known that You sent Me**. And I have declared to them Your name, and will declare it, that the love with which You loved Me may be in them, and I in them."—John 17:24-26*

The Father Sent Jesus, So Jesus Carried His Authority

Jesus carried authority with Him and passed it on to us.

"And [Jesus] said to them, 'I saw Satan fall like lightning from heaven. Behold, I give you the authority to trample on serpents and scorpions, and over all the power of the enemy, and nothing shall by any means hurt you.'"—Luke 10:18-19

When the church sends ministers, they carry the authority that Jesus gave the church. Churches equip saints through the fivefold, then send them out. They have authority over all the power of the enemy to cleanse cities and restore God's glory.

Jesus, the Sent One, Came to Send Us as His Ambassadors

God sent Jesus. Jesus, the Sent One, sends us.

Christ is in us and we know the Father sent Him

*"I in them, and You in Me; that they may be made perfect in one, and **that the world may know that You have sent Me**, and have loved them as You have loved Me. Father, I desire that they also whom You gave Me may be with Me where I am, that they may behold My glory which You have given Me; for You loved Me before the foundation of the world. O righteous Father! The world has not known You, but I have known You; and **these have known that You sent Me**."*
—John 17: 23 25

We are His ambassadors. God sends us and speaks through us

*"Now then, **we are ambassadors for Christ**, as though God were pleading through us: we implore you on Christ's behalf, be reconciled to God. For He made Him who knew no sin to be sin for us, that we might become the righteousness of God in Him."*
—2 Corinthians 5:20-21

Jesus Was Sent to Be Slain and Is Worthy of All Honor

While you might like to think of Jesus all shiny and picture-perfect now, God sees the end from the beginning. Jesus is disfigured. He has holes in His hands and His feet because He is the Lamb slain from the foundation of the world. He's sitting in glory as if the Resurrection has already happened. Jesus is sitting on the throne, and He looks the way He looked on Calvary. His appearance before the Father is in remembrance of what He did.

> *"And I looked, and behold, in the midst of the throne and of the four living creatures, and in the midst of the elders, **stood a Lamb as though it had been slain**, having seven horns and seven eyes, which are the seven Spirits of God sent out into all the earth. Then He came and took the scroll out of the right hand of Him who sat on the throne.*
>
> *"Now when He had taken the scroll, the four living creatures and the twenty-four elders fell down before the Lamb, each having a harp, and golden bowls full of incense, which are the prayers of the saints. And they sang a new song, saying:*
>
> > *"'**You are worthy** to take the scroll,*
> > *And to open its seals;*
> > *For You were slain,*
> > *And have redeemed us to God by Your blood*
> > *Out of every tribe and tongue and people and nation,*
> > *And have made us kings and priests to our God;*
> > *And we shall reign on the earth.'"*
> > *—Revelation 5:6-10*

Jesus became manifest for you

> *"He indeed was foreordained before the foundation of the world, but was manifest in these last times **for you**."—1 Peter 1:20*

4. Jesus Sent the Apostles

"And Jesus came and spoke to them, saying, 'All authority has been given to Me in heaven and on earth.

"'Go therefore and make disciples of all the nations, baptizing them in the name of the Father and of the Son and of the Holy Spirit, teaching them to observe all things that I have commanded you; and lo, I am with you always, even to the end of the age.' Amen."—Matthew 28:18-20

J esus spent most of His time equipping and sending disciples, not preaching to mass congregations and grand country sides of people. He focused on the few He had chosen to be equipped and sent.

Yes, Jesus fed 5,000, but they were not the ones where He placed His confidence. Most of the 5,000 just went home.

He healed ten lepers, but only one said thank you.

Friends dropped a man through the roof for Jesus to heal him. The Bible says that when they left, all the people who witnessed the healing went their way.

Jesus Focused on Those Who Could Be Sent

Jesus focused on equipping men whom He could Send. After His resurrection, He commissioned them to go and make disciples of nations. In John 17, He tied together the Sent Ones with Himself and with the Father in His prayer:

> *"As You sent Me into the world, I also have sent them into the world."—John 17:18*

The Sender and Those He Sends Are United by Love

Jesus' Father was the Sender, and Jesus was the One Sent. They were united by love. When the fivefold are the senders and their disciples are the Sent, they are also united by love. Jesus' apostles became spiritual fathers to their generation. We are their descendants. In our generation, pastors are also fathers who equip sons and daughters and send them out. They are united with the Sent Ones and with the Lord with cords of love. Fathers are unified, in one accord, and in fellowship, as Jesus prayed—"that they may be one as We are."

> *"Now I am no longer in the world, but these are in the world, and I come to You. Holy Father, keep through Your name those whom You have given Me, **that they may be one as We are**."—John 17:11*

One of the 12 Apostles Was Disqualified. He Was Never Sent.

Among the original 12 whom Jesus equipped, 11 were Sent but one was Disqualified—Judas, "the son of perdition."

> *"While I was with them in the world, I kept them in Your name. Those whom You gave Me I have kept; and none of them is lost except the son of perdition, that the Scripture might be fulfilled."—John 17: 12*

Throughout this book you will continue to see three groups of people—the Sent, the Removed, and the Disqualified.

Reinstatement of the Number Twelve

Jesus had 12 disciples until Judas was Disqualified. Then He had 11. The apostles chose Matthias and the number of disciples became 12 again (*Acts 1:26*). In the Bible the number 12 is important. Here are some examples from Revelation 21:

*"Also she had a great and high wall with **twelve gates**, and **twelve angels** at the gates, and names written on them, which are the names of the **twelve tribes** of the children of Israel: three gates on the east, three gates on the north, three gates on the south, and three gates on the west.*

*"Now the wall of the city had **twelve foundations**, and on them were the names of the **twelve apostles** of the Lamb."—Revelation 21:12-14*

Apostles Always Sought More Disciples to Equip and Send

It is important to note how the 12 apostles occupied themselves. They were preaching, teaching, and writing but mainly they pursued fresh new disciples they could equip and Send. They weren't gathering great crusades with crowds of people who would simply walk away. No. They focused on multiplication and lasting transformation by equipping and sending leaders. They evaluated potential candidates to decide who could be Sent and made decisions when some had to be Removed or Disqualified.

History of Apostles Is History of Equipping and Sending

The church in the book of Acts was constantly equipping and sending leaders to spread the Gospel and multiply the church. These leaders, in turn, would grow the church by equipping and sending more leaders. And it became a continuum.

The Gospel is about God's people becoming disciples who can be equipped to become the Sent.

This Gospel has to be re-looked at, re-approached.
We need to be training leaders.
We need to be training missionaries.
We need to be training people.

Paul Knew He Should Be Sent by the Church

Although Paul was called to preach by a personal encounter with Jesus, he still submitted his teachings to the leading apostles in the Jerusalem church. He was already teaching the gospel of grace to the Gentiles, but he understood that he was not acting alone. He was part of one church, the Body of Christ.

So Paul went to the leaders—James, Peter and John—and said, "Listen, I'm preaching about grace. I want you guys to judge what I am teaching to make sure that it's OK with you." They recognized that his gift was from God and accepted him as their fellow worker.

> *". . . and when James, Cephas, and John, who seemed to be pillars, perceived the grace that had been given to me, they gave me and Barnabas the right hand of fellowship, that we should go to the Gentiles and they to the circumcised."*—Galatians 2:9

Great Equippers Like Paul Need Great Courage

In 2 Corinthians 11: 22-33, the Apostle Paul describes 22 times that he paid the price for equipping the saints with the Gospel of Jesus Christ. He faced perils of waters, perils of robbers, was beaten with rods, once stoned, three times shipwrecked. Paul was beat up and dealt with, yet he was still willing to go on.

Because of Paul's faith and courage, God used him to become the greatest Equipper of the saints that we've ever known. He wrote most of the New Testament. He could not have written it with the same intensity without those trials.

Equipping Saints Means Equipping People Who Are Holy

The term *saint* is used 93 times in the New Testament. We're called believers and we're called a lot of other things, but in the Bible originally *saint* was used to define the church or God's people more often than any other term. The word *saint* was removed in the 1600s at the time the King James version was translated. Some modern versions put it back and there is some balancing of the term in different translations. It's a shame, because that word defines this group of people who are the saints of God that Paul was equipping.

The word *saint* relates to holiness

Saint relates to holiness. It has to do with a call. It has to do with divine purpose. It has to do with a lot of areas that the saints stepped into and qualified for.

> *"To the church of God which is at Corinth, to those who are sanctified in Christ Jesus, called to be saints, with all who in every place call on the name of Jesus Christ our Lord, both theirs and ours."*
> —1 Corinthians 1:2

Equip and Send Is Just as Vital as Pastoral Care

A lot of guys used to think that the only way you got into ministry is to say you would be a pastor. It was like the entrance.

I have a prophetic gift and apostolic ministry and I happen to pastor a church. In that process I have others on staff around us who are pastoring the flock. But I've never been a pastor. It's not my declaration.

There will always be a need for pastoral care, but the churches with the greatest effectiveness in fulfilling the Great Commission focus on equipping and sending saints. Jesus is our example. Those He sent changed the world. Let's keep it going.

5. Some Ministries Were Not Sent, They Just Went

"Then some of the itinerant Jewish exorcists took it upon themselves to call the name of the Lord Jesus over those who had evil spirits, saying, 'We exorcise you by the Jesus whom Paul preaches.' Also there were seven sons of Sceva, a Jewish chief priest, who did so.
"And the evil spirit answered and said, 'Jesus I know, and Paul I know; but who are you?'
"Then the man in whom the evil spirit was leaped on them, overpowered them, and prevailed against them, so that they fled out of that house naked and wounded."—Acts 19:13-16

Sometimes at our Peace for the City pastors' meetings in Baltimore I have met younger guys who say they want to start a parachurch ministry. I don't find parachurches anywhere in the Scriptures. I don't see any history of them anywhere in the Gospels. These guys claim to have inspiration from God, but they are not following the biblical example of equipping and sending that we see in Jesus and the apostles.

Some of the gray-haired bishops, apostles, and prophets come around to these pastors' meetings to pass the baton to the younger generation *in the churches*. That is an important distinction, *in the churches*. Church leaders represent biblical authority and generational continuity. They have something often missing in the parachurch—biblical equipping and sending. This disconnect becomes clear when the fivefold are equipping leaders but have to Remove or Disqualify a potential leader. Then he goes out on his own to start a ministry as an act of rebellion.

I've never been a proponent of the parachurch movement. The prefix "para" reminds me of the word parasite, and I don't believe that God shows us in the Book of Acts that there were ever parasite ministries outside the church.

It's No Mystery Why Startups Choose a Parachurch Model

After decades in ministry, it is no mystery to me why startups choose parachurch or independent ministry. They don't want the requirements and accountability of church government.

Nobody can tell them anything. As a result, they breed a rebellious attitude that spills over on those who come around them, because kind produces kind. They breed people who don't want anybody giving them advice.

Churches have been destroyed when an arrogant youth pastor arises and divides the people. Self-promoting music leaders have broken off and taken members with them. It happens all over. When you separate yourself from the church to start a parachurch ministry, you are placing yourself outside the covering of the local church. Often you are outside the covering of God.

Parachurch Can Become a License for Rebellion

Equipping and sending are essential for Christian growth and development. The local church is where babies are dedicated, marriages are performed, funerals are held, and people are equipped as the Sent who start churches and ministries.

Before leaders become Sent, they are trained and qualified. They are equipped with sound doctrine and approved by fathers who continue to support them spiritually after they leave.

Parachurch groups do damage to the body of Christ when they become a license for rebellion. When they reject covering, discipline, and structure and just want to do their own thing, many times they end up in tragedy. They end up hurting other ministries.

Everybody Needs the Covering of a Pastor

I believe very strongly if you're in ministry, if you're in business or government, if you're a born-again believer, you should have a pastor. You should have a covering. I don't really care who doesn't think it fits. I'm giving you the biblical position.

Jesus Said If You Give Yourself Honor, It's Worthless

Jesus did not glory in being independent. He declared many times throughout His lifetime that He was sent by His Father. He warned those who seek their own glory instead of giving glory to the one who sent them. He said if you give yourself honor, that honor is worth nothing at all.

> *"He who speaks from himself seeks his own glory; but He who seeks the glory of the One who sent Him is true, and no unrighteousness is in Him."—John 7:18*

> *"And I do not seek My own glory; there is One who seeks and judges."—John 8:50*

> *"Jesus answered, 'If I honor Myself, My honor is nothing. It is My Father who honors Me, of whom you say that He is your God.'"—John 8:54*

> *"And no man takes this honor to himself, but he who is called by God, just as Aaron was.*
> *"So also Christ did not glorify Himself to become High Priest, but it was He who said to Him:*
> *"'You are My Son,*
> *Today I have begotten You.'"—Hebrews 5:1-5*

Jesus Will Return for a Glorious Church, Not a Parachurch

Independent churches and parachurch ministries can come unglued and fall apart. People get disappointed and frustrated and pastors quit the ministry. Often they were not Sent. They just went.

The greatest hindrance to one unified and victorious church transforming cities everywhere is the disunity and disassociation of churches and ministries in a city. They won't work together to guard the city and protect the peace of God.

Sometimes the pastors are young upstarts who went out to pastor churches but weren't Sent. They carried a lousy attitude against their pastor and started a competing work that brought division to the whole city. That's why you see little churches scattered all over the place in cities. They don't grow and don't work together and so the cities are descending into darkness.

One night at a conference in Nigeria, I asked this question: If Jesus showed up in this country, which church would He choose to show up in? Some were tempted to say mine, but they didn't.

Jesus didn't trust human nature. Trust is a process. We earn His trust by doing ministry in one accord, God's way.

Section 2.
Equipping the Saints

6. Equip, Multiply, and Unify the Church

"And with many other words he testified and exhorted them, saying, 'Be saved from this perverse generation.' Then those who gladly received his word were baptized; and that day about three thousand souls were added to them."
—Acts 2:40-41

A young man and his wife who live in North Carolina were under the ministry of Charles Green. After Pastor Green was no longer there, they reached out to me, so I worked with them. I helped them solve a major problem that could have been catastrophic. I gave them some wisdom about a way to handle it and they followed my advice. Because they carried themselves well, some positive things are happening. I'm going to continue to help them so that they can continue to be Equippers.

Equippers are senior leaders in the church who prepare people to be sent out to do ministry.

You don't hear many Sunday messages about the need to be equipped and sent. You hear talks about how to improve your spiritual health, who you are as your real self, how to grow into a better person, but in my opinion, we don't have enough teachings about Equippers who equip the saints as the Sent in ministry.

The Bible places the whole context of the believer's life into being equipped and Sent. It is not doing your own thing. You represent Christ and the church, not yourself. That is the opposite of the way the world sees it. In the world, which the Bible calls "this perverse generation," the way to success is to climb the proverbial ladder and step on everybody on your way up. In the Kingdom, the way up is down. God wants us to multiply and fill the earth, but He wants us to do it His way. Things in the world don't translate to things in the church.

Constantly Multiplying Sent Ones in the Early Church

Following God's divine order, the early church went from 12 disciples to 70 to 120 in the Upper Room to 3,000 at Pentecost to 5,000 by Acts 4:4. This all took place under persecution because the church came together—often secretly—to be equipped by the fivefold ministry and sent out. They multiplied in trials, reaching nations, because disciples were being equipped and sent.

Assets of the Early Church

When these assets of the early church are missing today, it weakens the church:

- Centrality of Jesus Christ and the Word
- Unity of faith
- Release of the Holy Spirit
- Vital role of Equippers
- Separating the Sent from the Removed and Disqualified
- Holiness of the saints and standards of godliness
- Christlike character requirements of disciples-in-training
- Christian response to persecution
- Awareness of spiritual warfare and success against it
- Fellowship of the saints, giving honor to those in authority

The Gospel and the teaching of the Word are vitally important to counter the noise and confusion of this day. The enemy is not bothered by simple church attendance, or even the lack of it. He's bothered when you dare to believe God and believe His Word and decide to give your life to God and do everything to advance the Kingdom through the church.

When even the church doesn't believe God, people are falling into pits and valleys of all sorts. We occupy too much of our time in church with things that have no eternal significance.

The Sent are the most important investment a local church can make. So don't be preoccupied with needs and people unqualified to be sent. Focus on the Equippers and the Sent.

7. Five Types of Equippers

"And He Himself gave some to be apostles, some prophets, some evangelists, and some pastors and teachers. for the equipping of the saints for the work of ministry."
—Ephesians 4:11

The church is a spiritual building and the chief cornerstone is the Lord Jesus Christ. It is built on the foundation of apostles and prophets. The fivefold who equip the saints to be Sent are apostles, prophets, evangelists, pastors, and teachers.

Fivefold Are United by Faith and a Common Mission

The spiritual building called the church consists of people on a mission. The true church is not a physical building but people in the process of being equipped, fitted together, and growing into a holy temple, a dwelling place of God in the Spirit.

"Jesus Christ Himself being the chief cornerstone, in whom the whole building, being fitted together, grows into a holy temple in the Lord, in whom you also are being built together for a dwelling place of God in the Spirit."—Ephesians 2:20-22

The construction of this holy temple involves an equipping process for future ministry. That's why all churches need a Bible school or at least systematic training in the Bible and its application to all of life. Whether you set people into the fivefold ministry or send them out into marketplace ministry, everyone should submit to be trained by your church's Equippers.

"Therefore humble yourselves under the mighty hand of God, that He may exalt you in due time."
—1 Peter 5:6

Humble Yourself and Submit to God and the Fivefold

The Bible says to humble yourself under the mighty hand of God so that in due season He will exalt you. This humility includes giving honor to senior leaders.

"Likewise you younger people, submit yourselves to your elders. Yes, all of you be submissive to one another, and be clothed with humility, for

"'God resists the proud,
But gives grace to the humble.'

"Therefore humble yourselves under the mighty hand of God, that He may exalt you in due time, casting all your care upon Him, for He cares for you."
—1 Peter 5:5-7

The Equipper humbles himself to seek God in the midst of trials, pressures, and attacks. Every demon in hell wants to prevent the Equipper from accomplishing God's purposes. However, these experiences empower him to train others to exercise authority against the devil by humbly yielding to God.

Fivefold Is Not Responsible for Giving You a Better Life

How did the church ever become a dispenser of advice on a better life? Why do its members demand this advice or leave?

The church has taken Scriptures and tied them together to give the illusion that God is only interested in making people feel good. God is not saying that at all. That's why we need Equippers who teach us how to be real Christians.

Fivefold See Three Types of People During the Equipping

The Equipper needs to understand he will encounter three types of people who potentially come to be equipped.

Not many training manuals cover these three types of people—Sent, Removed, and Disqualified. That is why I wrote this book.

I hope this book becomes a tool for pastors and leaders who equip the saints for the work of ministry.

Here again are the three groups:

> *The Sent.* Only this group is qualified to be sent out. The other two groups will be delayed or never sent.
>
> *The Removed.* These resist Equipping and cannot be sent until they are put on hold for another day in the hope that they will humble themselves, repent, and grow in God.
>
> *The Disqualified.* These are people we prevent from stepping into the ministry arena because they lack the right character, knowledge, or spiritual commitment. If you let the blind lead the blind, both will fall in the ditch.

Fivefold Equip Church to Make Disciples of All Nations

The church exists to make disciples. The church equips the saints to be unified in the faith and the knowledge of Jesus, being perfected to become fully like Christ.

> *". . . for the edifying of the body of Christ, till we all come to the unity of the faith and of the knowledge of the Son of God, to a perfect man, to the measure of the stature of the fullness of Christ."—Ephesians 4:12b-13*

The Church Is Built on Apostle and Prophet, Not Pastor

The Bible says you build the church on the foundation of the apostle and prophet. Those who build the church in any other way are not building it correctly.

> *". . . fellow citizens with the saints and members of the household of God, having been built on the foundation of the apostles and prophets."*—Ephesians 2:19-20

The apostle sets everything in order. That's like the thumb on your hand. It can touch all the other ministries, represented by the fingers on your hand.

The prophet brings the declarations and decrees from the Old and New Testament.

All five of the fivefold are senior leaders—apostle, prophet, evangelist, pastor, teacher. They all have roles in equipping the saints to become the Sent. The Bible says these leaders are God's gift to the church.

Fivefold Ministry—Senior Leaders in the Church

Apostle ▪ Prophet ▪ Evangelist ▪ Pastor ▪ Teacher

". . . for the equipping of the saints for the work of ministry."—Ephesians 4:11

Every Church Needs a Bible School or Bible Curriculum

During my 40 years in Baltimore, we have established a Bible school to train people for community ministry, the workplace, and the marketplace, as well as the House of the Lord. Sometimes students enroll in Bible school after they graduate from high school, college, or premed, for a Gap Year.

Everyone uses their studies to grow closer to God and evaluate the direction of their lives.

8. Character Qualities of an Equipper

"Uzziah was sixteen years old when he became king. . . And he did what was right in the sight of the Lord, according to all that his father Amaziah had done."—2 Chronicles 26:3, 4

Uzziah did what was right in the sight of the Lord. That summarizes a key character quality of an Equipper.

Uzziah was raised as the child of a king and his father followed the Lord, at least some of the time. In 2 Chronicles 25 the Bible says of Uzziah's father Amaziah, *"And he did what was right in the sight of the Lord, but not with a loyal heart."*

Amaziah died when his son Uzziah was 16. Do you remember when you were 16? Some of you, I wouldn't have trusted you with a bag of peanuts, and you wouldn't have trusted me at 16. Some of you were running after your girlfriend, some of you were playing sports, some of us were doing drugs at 16. Man, we couldn't have ruled a city, much less a nation.

Uzziah Was Raised in the Household of a King

However, Uzziah had been raised in the environment of a king's household, so knew protocol, much like Charles III, who became king upon the death of his mother, Queen Elizabeth, and was anointed king in a coronation ceremony in London.

Uzziah knew processes. This boy had been equipped. He had been taught by his father to become king one day.

> *"And he did what was right in the sight of the Lord, according to all that his father Amaziah had done."*
> *—2 Chronicles 26:3*

Uzziah Was Raised with the Counsel of a Prophet

Uzziah's Equippers were his father and the prophet Zechariah.

"He sought God in the days of Zechariah, who had understanding in the visions of God."—2 Chronicles 26:5

He sought God. The Bible says Uzziah *"sought God in the days of Zechariah."* The Bible said Zechariah understood visions of God. The Hebrew word for *sought* suggests that Uzziah asked questions. He diligently inquired. He pursued frequently. He worshipped. He asked God for help. And it says God miraculously blessed him, favored him, and prospered him.

Uzziah Prospered as Long as He Sought the Lord

". . . and as long as he sought the Lord, God made him prosper."—2 Chronicles 26:5

Beginning at age 16, Uzziah was responsible for handling his nation's economy, unemployment, inflation, war, and other major issues. Let's bring it up to date and add to this young man's kingly duties immigration, border control, crime, national aggressions from Russia, Iran, China. Pandemics, energy issues, political issues. Perhaps he could have handled those, too, because he was a man who prospered because he sought the Lord.

Uzziah Became Famous and Strong

"Then Uzziah prepared for them, for the entire army, shields, spears, helmets, body armor, bows, and slings to cast stones. And he made devices in Jerusalem, invented by skillful men, to be on the towers and the corners, to shoot arrows and large stones. So his fame spread far and wide, for he was marvelously helped till he became strong."—2 Chronicles 26:14-15

Uzziah made devices, used his intellect, used the arts, and used giftings and technology. He had devices in Jerusalem that were made by many talented men and placed them in towers on the corners of the wall to shoot large arrows and large stones. He was still only a teenager. Think about that.

Let's look at the pathways where God led King Uzziah.

God enabled Uzziah to go to war. He broke down walls and built cities right in front of the Philistine enemy.

> *"Now he went out and made war against the Philistines, and broke down the wall of Gath, the wall of Jabneh, and the wall of Ashdod; and he built cities around Ashdod and among the Philistines."*
> —*2 Chronicles 26:6*

Remember, some of these Philistines were giants. Yet Uzziah built right in the middle of the enemy's territory. People were so impressed with what he was able to do that they gave gifts to Uzziah and his name spread throughout all of Judah, even to the gates of Egypt. He built towers. He conquered cities and lands, reestablished them, and rebuilt them.

Don't Fail Like Uzziah—Never Stop Seeking the Lord

We know that in the end Uzziah failed when he became proud and stopped seeking the Lord. When you are an Equipper, you have people following you. You don't have that option. Keep following the Lord. Your life and the lives of those following you depend on your faithfulness to keep seeking. Remember the words of Paul:

> *"Be ye followers of me, even as I also am of Christ."*
> —*1 Corinthians 11:1 KJV*

If I'm not following the Lord, don't follow me, but if I am, follow me as I follow the Lord. You should be able to say, "He sought the Lord and found the correct way to handle that."

9. Prayer Life of an Equipper

"Therefore I take pleasure in infirmities, in reproaches, in needs, in persecutions, in distresses, for Christ's sake. For when I am weak, then I am strong."—2 Corinthians 12:10

One time in New York City a great move of God was taking place and people were being healed. On one particular night, the man who was running the meetings believed God would do even greater miracles.

A loud man came and sat in the front row. He was drunk and had brought his little son with him who had spina bifida, a hole in his spine. The boy's little legs were skinny and he couldn't even use them to walk. The preacher saw them and said to himself, *My God, this man is going to cause trouble tonight.*

The drunken man started yelling, "This man is a fake! If he was real, my son would be healed!" He kept yelling and finally picked up his son and held him in the air saying, "If you are real and your God is real, heal my son!"

The preacher fell on his knees on the floor of the stage. With his face in his hands, he cried out to the Lord, "God, I'm done! I can't heal this boy. I'm done. I can't do it. God, I'm finished. I can't do it anymore. I can't heal unless you heal, God. I can't do a thing and this little boy needs to be healed."

The next thing he knew, this little boy's legs began to fly in the air as if he were pedaling a bicycle. The father couldn't control him so he rushed up and put him on the stage. Then the little boy started running around the stage. He went over and hugged the preacher's legs and held on to him, and the Glory of God came in that meeting as God healed that boy.

Equippers Pray in Their Weakness

God is going to raise up humble people who are willing to say, "Lord, I can't do this." Even when you are weak you can still be anointed. When you feel weak you can be strong in God!

Equippers Pray Against Opposition

The devil is not happy when you equip people to pray. Early in the book of Acts, Satan is found opposing the people and the purpose of God.

Satan is opposed to the message of the Equipper because he's opposed to the Sent Ones getting equipped for the work of the ministry by learning how to pray.

Unsaved people will also oppose you. They are not happy when people pray.

Your own members may reject you when you set standards of consistent prayer for the whole church.

All things pertaining to the equipping of the saints for the work of the ministry to build up the body of Christ have a cost and require you to enter a battleground you have never entered before. It costs me every day.

Equippers Pray for Discernment About Deceitful Workers

"For such are false apostles, deceitful workers, transforming themselves into apostles of Christ. And no wonder! For Satan himself transforms himself into an angel of light. Therefore it is no great thing if his ministers also transform themselves into ministers of righteousness, whose end will be according to their works."—2 Corinthians 11:13-15

The Equipper knows that everyone who walks in the doors of the church is not a sincere seeker after truth. The Bible says that some are false apostles and deceitful workers. Behind them is Satan himself.

Equippers need spiritual discernment, so they seek the mind of God *before* placing people in positions of authority and influence. If you don't pray first and get God's direction, it's hard to get people out once you have put them in those positions.

Equippers have to get out the Gospel without the confusion of the Disqualified or those who should be Removed so they ask God about everything. Their hours in prayer reach an all-time level of intercession to fulfill their calling to equip the Sent.

Equippers Stay Above Their Problems Through Prayer

An Equipper is a watchman. Prayer gives him the ability to remain above daily problems. One example from the Old Testament of staying above daily issues is the towers of Uzziah. Those towers represent the prayers of a watchman.

> *"And Uzziah built towers in Jerusalem at the Corner Gate, at the Valley Gate, and at the corner buttress of the wall; then he fortified them. Also he built towers in the desert. He dug many wells, for he had much livestock, both in the lowlands and in the plains; he also had farmers and vinedressers in the mountains and in Carmel, for he loved the soil."*
> *—2 Chronicles 26:9-10*

Uzziah built towers everywhere, including on the walls of Jerusalem. He built small, sheltered towers in the vineyards. He built towers in the fields and had them elevated so that watchmen could look down on the harvest. Watchmen could spot the foxes that spoil the vines. Parents could climb into the towers to find their children who were playing in the fields. During harvest time, the whole family would often live in those towers.

Towers in the Old Testament were a symbol of protection from enemies and thieves, rising above the process. The tower was a place to restore and store your supplies. The tower was a symbol of strength, visibility, and protection. You see the harvest. You find out how to protect it. And you rest.

Prayer Was the Secret of David's Strength

When David prayed, he entered a tower of the Lord's strength. Inside the Lord's tower, David was above his enemy. He could see reality again because he had the Lord's perspective.

"My lovingkindness and my fortress,
My high tower and my deliverer,
My shield and the One in whom I take refuge,
Who subdues my people under me."—Psalm 144:2

"For in the time of trouble
He shall hide me in His pavilion;
In the secret place of His tabernacle
He shall hide me;
He shall set me high upon a rock."—Psalm 27:5

Why the Devil Has Started Paying Attention to You

The devil is the Christian's adversary, but some people in church never had the devil pay any attention to them even one time, because they aren't doing anything. But an Equipper facing down the devil in the strength of the Lord gets his attention. He's a real threat.

When I was in the gangs, I was a fighter and a boxer and I was mean as a snake. I wasn't worried about the guy over in the corner sucking his thumb. I was worried about the guy who was looking straight at me, eyeball to eyeball. That's the guy I had to worry about.

Don't worry about the devil. Jesus has already taken care of him. Stare him down in the authority of Jesus. Send him away.

10. Father's Heart of an Equipper

"For though you might have ten thousand instructors in Christ, yet you do not have many fathers; for in Christ Jesus I have begotten you through the gospel."—1 Corinthians 4:15

When my wife and I came to Baltimore, my spiritual father Pastor John Gimenez came and gave a little speech to the handful of people who were with us to plant a church. He told them, "Take care of him. He is a gift." Then he said, "If you don't take care of him, I'm coming up here to see you, and I'll take him home."

That day never came because I behaved myself. I followed God. I knew the Word. The fivefold at Rock Church had equipped me and I took to heart my responsibilities as a son and a Christian.

Father/Son Relationships in the Fear of God

God wants to raise up spiritual fathers who will walk before God humbly and train and equip another generation, but God will hold both fathers and sons accountable. If the fathers fail to serve the Lord until the end, then I tell you what God will do. He'll judge the fathers. And if the sons fail to walk after God, even though the fathers stumbled, God won't let them succeed.

We need to remember the fear of God in this day. God is looking for daughters and sons who will submit themselves to a father spirit in the fear of the Lord. When that happens correctly, both the father and the son become joined in such a way that God is glorified through both the father's life and the son's life.

Beware of Arrogance Against Fathers

In 1980, I was at the forefront of one of the biggest youth movements happening in America. John Gimenez led Washington for Jesus where 500,000 people from all over America came to the Washington Mall. At that time, we also put together one of the largest youth meetings that had ever been held in America—33,000 kids at RFK Stadium the day before. From there, God gave us a platform with voices of many of the people you know.

Beginning in 1999, we worked with Lou Engle to bring 300,000 youth to The Call in Washington, DC. We brought the stage, put it up, tore it down, and served in the best capacity we could to keep things running smoothly. Guys like Sean Voight were raised up at that time and other great new preachers.

Many of those young leaders came together later at a hotel in Dallas, Texas. I was invited to come, and I sat in the opening session with this group of guys. They were all sharing how they heard God and they were going to take the mantle and run with it, and they were going to do all these new things.

The Spirit of God rose up in me. I knew all of them by name and they knew me. I said to them, "Dear brothers, I want to say to you that this is arrogance. This is nothing but pride. This is not the plan of God. God did not raise you up to grab that mantle. He raised you up for the mantle to fall on you. You're not going to grab anything, and if you do, God will cause it to come back on your head and you will suffer like Uzziah if you take this out of context."

"But when [Uzziah] was strong his heart was lifted up, to his destruction, for he transgressed against the LORD his God by entering the temple of the LORD to burn incense on the altar of incense. . . . King Uzziah was a leper until the day of his death. He dwelt in an isolated house, because he was a leper; for he was cut off from the house of the Lord."
—2 Chronicles 26:17,21

Then I got up and walked out and went to my hotel room. I got on my bed and just lay there. My heart was broken.

"Lord, what in the world? How could these young men even think of such a thing?"

Then I began to hear a knock on my door and then another knock and another and another and another until there was nowhere left in my room to stand.

These young leaders came in and said, "My God, man, we are so wrong, and we repent."

Even though that meeting had been announced, programs printed, and things set up all over the place, it was shut down and they never had another meeting.

Novices Need Spiritual Fathers

When you don't understand the deeper things of the workings of God, you misjudge the actions of senior church leaders because you are a novice. You are immature. You don't have the responsibilities of a spiritual father. You are a spectator. Your opinions are not based on prophetic insight.

I'm going to tell you something. We will see another generation of preachers, another generation of businessmen, another generation of young leaders coming to the scene. I am excited to be able to give them anything that God has given me. Freely I have received, so freely I give.

But I must say this. It will not be transferred to those who are rebellious, arrogant, and disrespectful to the fathers. I am appalled when I see young men who mock and joke about their own fathers who are raising them up. God will not allow a proud generation to come and stand in this next great day of revival and represent the body of Christ nor the King of Glory!

God Honored Jesus at His Baptism—"This is my Son"

"When all the people were baptized, it came to pass that Jesus also was baptized; and while He prayed, the heaven was opened.

"And the Holy Spirit descended in bodily form like a dove upon Him, and a voice came from heaven which said, 'You are My beloved Son; in You I am well pleased.'"—Luke 3:21-22

Listen, it's not often that you hear God speaking, overriding all the other aspects of creation. He doesn't often interfere, but here He speaks out of heaven till it rings like a loud noise and He says, *"Hey, this is my Son!"*

He let Satan know that. He let the disciples know that. He let everybody know that. God was showing that His Son would move through a series of processes to sit with Him in Heaven. But Jesus had to be a Son before all that could happen.

Jesus Always Honored His Father

Jesus always gave honor to His Father, including His prayer in John 17:

"Father, the hour has come. Glorify Your Son, that Your Son also may glorify You, as You have given Him authority over all flesh, that He should give eternal life to as many as You have given Him. And this is eternal life, that they may know You, the only true God, and Jesus Christ whom You have sent. I have glorified You on the earth. I have finished the work which You have given Me to do. And now, O Father, glorify Me together with Yourself, with the glory which I had with You before the world was."—John 17:1-5

Jesus is saying, in essence, "I have no words except the words that You gave Me for them. They have received them and know that I came from You and believe that You sent Me."

That's the attitude of a Son who is profitable for the Kingdom.

Equippers Who Are Fathers Begin as Sons

Two father/son principles work together that I believe strongly are correct church structure.

- An Equipper was once a son submitted to a father who prepared him for God's work.
- While the Equipper was a son, he also learned to be a father.

Prayer for Fathers and Sons

God, stir our hearts and stir up another generation of leaders who will step to the forefront and say with humility, "Thank God for fathers."

Yes, there are bad fathers, but also there are good fathers, and we need to honor fathers. You have many instructors, Paul said, but you don't have many fathers. We need fathers today—biblically based fathers, men who want to see sons become somebody great for the Kingdom. We need sons who are not puffed up and believing they are somebody but humbly admitting they need a father.

Just because some sons get hurt and wounded, that does not nullify the process. The sons need to repent if they have unforgiveness and put away any ugly wounds. Walk away from any offences and embrace the good fathers who want to raise you up, equip you, and see God anoint you and flow through you.

11. The Equipper's Anointing

"And it shall come to pass in that day, that his burden shall be taken away from off thy shoulder, and his yoke from off thy neck, and the yoke shall be destroyed because of the anointing."—Isaiah 10:27 KJV

Whether you're the Equipper or the Equipped, you can be anointed even when you are weak, if your weakness is not from sin but from humility.

When you're humbled by your weakness, the Lord is made strong in you. The tenderness of that process allows you to be humbled while you're anointed.

Most problems with anointing arise when you're strong and anointed. You make a fool of yourself and God by thinking and acting as if you did it all yourself.

Three Anointings of David to Be King

David was anointed three times—as future king, then king of Judah, and then king of all the tribes of Israel.

1. Anointed by Samuel *(1 Samuel 16:1-13)*

2. Anointed King over Judah *(2 Samuel 2:1-7)*

3. Anointed King over All Tribes of Israel *(2 Samuel 5:1-4)*

Five Battles of David Prepared Him to Be King

David fought five battles—a bear, a lion, a giant, the Philistine army, and the house of Saul.

1. David fought a bear *(1 Samuel 17:34-35)*.

2. David fought a lion *(1 Samuel 17:36)*.

3. David fought a giant *(1 Samuel 17:40-51)*.

4. David fought the Philistine Army *(1 Samuel 17:51-58)*.

5. The house of Saul fought against the house of David *(2 Samuel 3:1 and 5:3-5)*.

---

1. David fought a bear. A bear sneaks up when you least expect it and doesn't tell you he's coming. You will fight battles against enemies that you don't see coming. All of a sudden, they are on you before you can do anything. David beat that bear.

2. David fought a lion. A lion is an intimidating enemy. Lions are all about sound. When it roars, a small animal a mile away can be paralyzed in fear. The sound of his roar can make an elephant move. It's the accusing voice, the verbal attack. When you defeat a lion, you defeat vicious accusations against you.

3. David fought a giant. The giant enemy is bigger than you, louder than you, with weapons bigger than you. David defeated the giant with a rock. Jesus said, "Upon this rock of revelation I'll build my church and giants of hell shall not prevail against it" (*see Matthew 16:18*).

4. David fought the Philistine army. David defeated the army from the secret place of the presence of God that defeats all enemies. When the shadow of the Almighty came down, it overtook that big giant, and the giant and the army could not figure out how David got so big. God's presence overshadowed the whole army of the Philistines, and they ran for their lives. When you get in His presence, He'll defeat your biggest enemy.

*"He who dwells in the secret place of the Most High
Shall abide under the shadow of the Almighty.
I will say of the Lord, 'He is my refuge and my
fortress;
My God, in Him I will trust.'"—Psalm 91:1-2*

5. The house of Saul fought against the house of David.
Saul had tried to kill David many times, and after Saul's death
the house of Saul tried to retain the throne. However, God had
determined that David would be king and in the end he was.

*"Now there was a long war between the house of Saul
and the house of David. But David grew stronger and
stronger, and the house of Saul grew weaker and
weaker."—2 Samuel 3:1*

*"And they anointed David king over Israel. David was
thirty years old when he began to reign, and he reigned
forty years. In Hebron he reigned over Judah seven
years and six months, and in Jerusalem he reigned
thirty-three years over all Israel and Judah."
—2 Samuel 5:3-5*

**Four Things Equippers Need to Know About the
Anointing**

1. The anointing equips the Sent Ones with the Truth
   (1 John 2:20-22).

2. The anointing from the Holy One is the unction from God
   (1 John 2:20, 21, 26, 27).

3. The anointing is always connected to the nine gifts of the
   Spirit *(1 Corinthians 12:4-11).*

4. The anointing destroys yokes *(Isaiah 10:27).*

---

1. The anointing equips the Sent Ones with the Truth.

No anointing is more vital for an Equipper training
the Sent than standing up for the truth that Jesus is the Christ.

"But you have an anointing from the Holy One, and you know all things. I have not written to you because you do not know the truth, but because you know it, and that no lie is of the truth. Who is a liar but he who denies that Jesus is the Christ? He is antichrist who denies the Father and the Son."—1 John 2:20-22

2. The anointing from the Holy One is the unction from God.

The anointing teaches you as you abide in Him. God gives you permission to use His name and His Word to do great things for Him.

"But you have an anointing from the Holy One, and you know all things. I have not written to you because you do not know the truth, but because you know it, and that no lie is of the truth. . . . These things I have written to you concerning those who try to deceive you. But the anointing which you have received from Him abides in you, and you do not need that anyone teach you; but as the same anointing teaches you concerning all things, and is true, and is not a lie, and just as it has taught you, you will abide in Him."
—1 John 2:20, 21, 26, 27

3. The anointing is always connected to the nine gifts of the Spirit.

"There are diversities of gifts, but the same Spirit. There are differences of ministries, but the same Lord. And there are diversities of activities, but it is the same God who works all in all. But the manifestation of the Spirit is given to each one for the profit of all: for to one is given the word of wisdom through the Spirit, to another the word of knowledge through the same Spirit, to another faith by the same Spirit, to another gifts of healings by the same Spirit, to another the working of miracles, to another prophecy, to another discerning of spirits, to

another different kinds of tongues, to another the interpretation of tongues. But one and the same Spirit works all these things, distributing to each one individually as He wills."—1 Corinthians 12:4-11

4. The anointing destroys yokes.

"And it shall come to pass in that day, that his burden shall be taken away from off thy shoulder, and his yoke from off thy neck, and the yoke shall be destroyed because of the anointing."—Isaiah 10:27 KJV

Five Limitations on the Anointing

In some charismatic churches they say, "If you just got anointed, you could sing better *(or play better or do better)*. I believe in the anointing, yes, but the anointing doesn't cover all areas. We have abused the anointing. Here are five things that the anointing cannot do.

Five Limitations on the Anointing

1. The anointing cannot keep you from temptation, but it can deliver you from temptation
   (Hebrews 4:15, James 1:13-15).

2. The anointing does not prevent sickness from your body
   (2 Kings 13:14).

3. The anointing does not protect you from being hated
   (1 Samuel 30:6).

4. The anointing doesn't prevent mental or emotional weakness *(Romans 8:26, Isaiah 26:3).*

5. The anointing doesn't keep you from problems or keep you isolated, but it breaks the yokes *(Isaiah 10:27).*

---

1. The anointing cannot keep you from temptation, but it can deliver you from temptation.

Your Bible can help you overcome temptations, but it doesn't prevent them. Jesus was tempted in all ways, as we are, yet he never sinned.

> "For we do not have a High Priest who cannot sympathize with our weaknesses, but was in all points tempted as we are, yet without sin."—Hebrews 4:15 .

You're never tempted by God. You're drawn away by your own flesh.

> "Let no one say when he is tempted, "I am tempted by God"; for God cannot be tempted by evil, nor does He Himself tempt anyone. But each one is tempted when he is drawn away by his own desires and enticed. Then, when desire has conceived, it gives birth to sin; and sin, when it is full-grown, brings forth death."
> —James 1:13-15

You can be anointed and be tempted. When you're tempted and you don't give in to the temptation, it can be broken. That's what the anointing can do. It breaks the yokes. In the anointing you can be delivered from the temptation. Remember, it says in Isaiah 10:27 that it's a yoke-breaking anointing.

2. The anointing does not prevent sickness from your body.

Elisha died of sickness.

> "Elisha had become sick with the illness of which he would die. Then Joash the king of Israel came down to him, and wept over his face, and said, 'O my father, my father, the chariots of Israel and their horsemen!'"
> —2 Kings 13:14

One of Paul's disciples became ill during their travels in Greece and Paul had to leave him behind. Why couldn't Paul just pray for him? The anointing didn't break it. Just because you're anointed doesn't mean you won't get COVID, but if you do, the anointing could break the yoke so you don't die.

3. The anointing does not protect you from being hated.

Actually, those who are anointed always seem to have some people who hate them. When David and his men were exiled in the wilderness because of Saul's persecution, they returned to their base in Ziklag one day and found that the Amalekites had attacked and burned it, taking captive their wives and everyone else in the camp. David's men turned on David and spoke of stoning him, but in his weakness he turned to the Lord and found new strength.

"David strengthened himself in the Lord his God."
—1 Samuel 30:6

4. The anointing doesn't prevent mental or emotional weakness.

"Likewise the Spirit also helpeth our infirmities: for we know not what we should pray for as we ought: but the Spirit itself maketh intercession for us with groanings which cannot be uttered."—Romans 8:26 KJV.

That word *infirmity* is moral, emotional, or mental weakness. Your anointing may not prevent your mental issues, but when your mind is stayed on the Lord, the Word renews your strength, including the strength of your mind and emotions.

"You will keep him in perfect peace, Whose mind is stayed on You, Because he trusts in You."—Isaiah 26:3

5. The anointing doesn't keep you from problems or keep you isolated, but it breaks the yokes.

> *"And it shall come to pass in that day, that his burden shall be taken away from off thy shoulder, and his yoke from off thy neck, and the yoke shall be destroyed because of the anointing."*—Isaiah 10:27 KJV

Saints Equipped for Battle by the Fivefold

When the fivefold equips the saints for the work of ministry, the saints are equipped to do battle for the Lord. They rise up and defeat abortion. They rise up and defeat the ugly things said and done against the church and against humanity. They rise up to be a voice in the wilderness!

Section 3

What You Receive from an Anointed Equipper

12. A Heart for People

"When you give a dinner or a supper, do not ask your friends, your brothers, your relatives, nor rich neighbors, lest they also invite you back, and you be repaid. But when you give a feast, invite the poor, the maimed, the lame, the blind. And you will be blessed, because they cannot repay you; for you shall be repaid at the resurrection of the just."—Luke 14:12-14

If you're going to be equipped, you have to learn to have a heart for people, even people you don't like.

When I'm equipping somebody in my church, I expect them to want to be around people. They want loved ones saved. They want people of every race, color, and shape coming in.

When the Apostle Paul was speaking of his sacrifices and persecutions in 1 Corinthians 9:2, he said, *"For you are the seal of my apostleship."* *"You yourselves are proof that I am the Lord's apostle"* (NLT).

> *"If I am not an apostle to others, yet doubtless I am to you. For you are the seal of my apostleship in the Lord."—1 Corinthians 9:2*

The people in my church prove that God sent me to Baltimore. Somebody said in my office, "I'm so glad God sent you here." Praise the Lord! I have been here 40 years. Those whom I have equipped have picked up my anointing as the Equipper. They cannot help but get my heart.

That's why I say that the Removed or the Disqualified should never be Equippers because they cannot help but give out the negativity that's in them. *"For out of the abundance of the heart the mouth speaks"* (Matthew 12:34).

If you don't like people, you need to get out of ministry.

I have seen some people come into ministry for the purpose of control. That's really sad, because sometimes the people whom they are controlling have more anointing than they do. If you are equipping somebody by controlling them, you are taking the gift that God put in them and stifling it.

God sets down one and raises up another. We need to keep our hands and our mouth off what God is doing.

> *"But God is the judge: he putteth down one, and setteth up another."*—Psalm 75:7 KJV

We need to watch God use people and set them in the body as it pleases Him. Let Him elevate whomever He wants.

13. A Humble Attitude of Submission

". . . giving thanks always for all things to God the Father in the name of our Lord Jesus Christ, submitting to one another in the fear of God."—Ephesians 5:20-21

When you are being equipped as the Sent, you need a heart attitude of submission. I don't preach about submission. I show you what Jesus said in the Bible.

> *"Then Jesus answered and said to them, 'Most assuredly, I say to you, the Son can do nothing of Himself, but what He sees the Father do; for whatever He does, the Son also does in like manner.'"* —John 5:19

Before the Bible says in Ephesians 5:22, *"Wives, submit to your own husbands, as to the Lord,"* it says *"submitting to one another in the fear of God" (verse 21).* And it is followed by verse 25, *"Husbands, love your wives, just as Christ also loved the church and gave Himself for her."*

Your Submission Shows If You Are Being Properly Equipped

My own heart, my attitude, my will, my agenda is submission. The word "sub" means below, so when you are in submission, you're below the mission. You're helping the mission become what it's supposed to be. You're not in competition with the mission. You're in submission. You took the lowest seat when asked to come into a room.

It bothers me when people come into a meeting and look for the highest seat in the room. When I come into a meeting, even when I am there as the leader, I prefer to sit down in a low place.

When you have the right attitude toward the mission and you're in submission, you can be promoted. Submission is not based on your understanding. It shows your heart toward the Equipper.

Jesus said, "I'm doing what the Father sent me to do."

"For I have not spoken on My own authority; but the Father who sent Me gave Me a command, what I should say and what I should speak."—John 12:49

Jesus submitted Himself to His Father and He reminded us over and over again that His Father had sent Him. Jesus was the Sent One. He demonstrated the relationship of submission to equipping and then sending. He prayed it back to God in John 17.

Powerful Impact of Submission on the Church

Submission is a biblical prerequisite for the equipping process. You submit to leadership, leadership equips you, and then you can become the Sent. Once you are sent, you remember those who sent you and return often to seek their counsel. They help you with sound doctrine and give you the benefit of their wisdom in ministry.

Submission strengthens the church. Jesus said, "The Father and I are one." He is our example of how submission produces oneness. Oneness strengthens the church for full effect.

Submission increases effectiveness. Paul related submission and agreement with those who sent him to the effectiveness of his ministry.

Submission maintains fellowship and sound doctrine. My spiritual son Jim Kilmartin is a pastor, but he still calls me. Paul Tan calls me for confirmation, even though he's been in ministry 35 years. He says, "Bishop, I think I heard a word and this is what I'm going to preach." I'll listen and we'll talk a little bit and many times it's an Amen, that's a good word. And I ask, "Can I use that word, too?" And so there's a sharing because it's so important that we don't think we can just go out and do our own thing. We stay in one accord with one another and the Word.

14. Embracing Another Man's Vision

"And if you have not been faithful in what is another man's, who will give you what is your own?"—Luke 16:12

I grew up in Rock Church in the 1970s and John Gimenez equipped me to be a pastor before he sent me out. I had an office right next to his. One day when he was preaching in California, the Lord God put a burden on his heart to bring the church of Jesus Christ together according to John 17. We would fast and pray and take a stand for Jesus and the Word of God in Washington, DC, in April 1980.

I embraced his vision. I knew it was from the Lord. He designated me as National Youth Director for what became Washington for Jesus.

In April 1980, an outpouring of 500,000 people came to Washington for Jesus. National Christian leaders spoke on prayer and fasting, returning to the Lord, unity of the church, and a turnaround for the United States. When John Gimenez spoke he said, "We've learned that God is still the same yesterday, today, and forever. He hasn't ceased from his miraculous ways. We have learned that God has the answer. He truly can deliver." And He did. Many Christians credited major national changes to that unified prayer meeting in the Nation's Capital.

Equipped and Likeminded

In 2023, at dawn on Resurrection Day, I stood on the shore of Baltimore's Inner Harbor with pastors from many denominations. From our pastors' fellowship Peace for the City we had called people together to pray for a Baltimore miracle. Another movement called Proclaim also joined us. They had the same vision for proclaiming the Gospel to our city.

When I left to start my own ministry in 1973, I had embraced the vision of John Gimenez. We were likeminded in our pursuit of unity in the church. Therefore, in my new role it was natural for me to reach out to likeminded pastors and ministries—locally, nationally, and later internationally.

Paul said about his son Timothy, *"For I have no one like-minded, who will sincerely care for your state." (Philippians 2:20)* He was saying, "I have nobody like him. I have nobody who is that like-minded." Timothy had embraced another man's vision, that of his spiritual father, Paul.

Rewards in Your God Account Never Get Spent

". . . doing the will of God from the heart, with goodwill doing service, as to the Lord, and not to men, knowing that whatever good anyone does, he will receive the same from the Lord, whether he is a slave or free."—Ephesians 6:6-8

Whatever good you do, you will receive a reward from the Lord, so stop trying to get your reward from the earth. If you get your reward from the earth, you'll spend it, but if you get it from glory, you can't spend it. That deposit stays in your heavenly checking account, your eternal credit card. You can use it when you're 50, you can use it when you're 70, you can use it all the way going out to glory. It stays in your account. But when you get your reward from the world, you spend it and you ain't got nothing.

Test People Before You Entrust Them with Your Vision

"So David went on and became great, and the Lord of hosts was with him."—1 Chronicles 11:9

David was king, but he always had to deal with people under him whom he trusted but who proved disloyal to him and were not committed to the same vision.

People who are given influential positions but carry a spirit of betrayal also influence betrayal in others. Absalom, Joab, Judas were all able to betray their leaders because they were placed in areas of influence.

However, as I said in Chapter 9, the level of damage from betrayal is weakened in the absence of influence. That's why you don't put people in places of influence until you can test them to see if they are likeminded and not trying to position themselves above you.

Neither one of you needs applause. You are likeminded. You can embrace another man's vision.

15. Praying and Waging Spiritual Warfare

"If you have run with the footmen, and they have wearied you, Then how can you contend with horses? And if in the land of peace, In which you trusted, they wearied you, Then how will you do in the floodplain of the Jordan?"—Jeremiah 12:5

The Bible is amazing on the subject of horses. In Jeremiah 12:5, the Lord rebukes Jeremiah's impatience. He says, "Look, Jeremiah, if you get tired with guys on foot, how are you going to handle the guys on horses? And if you run with guys on foot in a land of peace—because the church always wants to be in peace—if you take flight in the land of peace, where you feel secure, then what will you do when you tread the tangled maze of jungle haunted by lions and the flooding of the Jordan?"

And what about COVID? That was a demonic attack, and if you quit now because of COVID, you'll never make it with the next thing that's coming.

Look how the church of today scattered when COVID hit. We need to understand the skill and art of war and not be terrified. We should move towards battle as a horse does.

Some of God's people are more interested in what discount they get at the restaurant where they eat on Sunday than what they are learning at church about spiritual warfare. They are focused on what they are going to do tonight instead of realizing you're in a battle that you have never, ever experienced.

Spiritual Attacks Increase When You're Anointed

"For Satan himself transforms himself into an angel of light. Therefore it is no great thing if his ministers also transform

themselves into ministers of righteousness, whose end will be according to their works."—2 Corinthians 11:14-15

Let me clarify a misunderstanding. People think that being anointed means that Satan can't come against you, but that's not true. That's foolishness, actually, because the attack intensifies when you're anointed.

People think the Holy Ghost protects them and they can walk along in a bubble where everything is blessed. The opposite is true. Instead, God takes you through a war zone where everybody and his mother is looking at you. Lying demons are talking about you at night when you go to bed. They are whispering in the eternals. They gather in the councils of hell and say, "Oh, we know how we can torment her. All we have to do is whisper lies to her and she'll believe what we tell her because she believes lies before she believes the truth."

Equippers Experience the Highest Level of Warfare

Warfare is at the highest level for the Equippers. I used to think it was intercessors, but I've changed my mind. The highest level of warfare is the Equipper, because he multiplies himself. The intercessor does not. The elder does not.

Paul Calls Out Elymas—"Son of the Devil"

The church at Antioch laid hands on Paul and Barnabas and sent them out, but Barnabas brought along John Mark as an assistant. He was not Sent, like Paul and Barnabas. They encountered spiritual warfare in Paphos.

The Bible says that the proconsul "sought to hear the word of the Lord," but Elymas, the sorcerer, kept interfering.

"Then Saul, who also is called Paul, filled with the Holy Spirit, looked intently at him and said, 'O full of all deceit and all fraud, you son of the devil, you enemy of all righteousness, will you not cease perverting the

straight ways of the Lord? And now, indeed, the hand of the Lord is upon you, and you shall be blind, not seeing the sun for a time.'"—Acts 13:9-11

What this guy Elymas came to do had been turned on him. When you're at a level that you speak a prophetic word and someone goes blind, some heavy spiritual activity is going on.

Coddling Your Church Doesn't Equip People for War

The church today has spent too much time coddling and caring for people instead of challenging and equipping them. Making people comfortable and feeling good instead of equipping them for the work of ministry is not biblical. It is essential to learn the skill of war. It is essential to learn spiritual warfare.

The senior leader has the burden of teaching the people how spiritual warfare is to be carried out because he's called to equip future leaders. Senior apostolic leaders should invest their time in equipping the Sent, but too many invest their time in nurturing people instead of developing leaders.

Churches attract weak people who have no intention of growing up. Three to five years later they are still coming to get blessed. They have no vision for making an impact on the world. They are not trying to be evangelists. They are not trying to do the work of the ministry. They are still trying to be coddled. Let me go to church so I can feel good. Somebody tell me good things about myself so I'll feel real good.

Spiritual Warfare Intensifies for the Sent

"Finally, my brethren, be strong in the Lord and in the power of His might. Put on the whole armor of God, that you may be able to stand against the wiles of the devil. For we do not wrestle against flesh and blood, but against principalities, against powers, against the rulers of the darkness of this age, against spiritual hosts of wickedness in the heavenly places.

Therefore take up the whole armor of God, that you may be able to withstand in the evil day, and having done all, to stand."—Ephesians 6:10-13

The Sent is not just somebody who is favored or really liked with a great charismatic personality. This whole sending thing intensifies because of the anointing.

In Jude it says when Michael contended with the devil he said, *"The Lord rebuke you!"* That archangel was saying, "I have to defer to God against this one, this fallen angel called Satan."

> *"Yet Michael the archangel, in contending with the devil, when he disputed about the body of Moses, dared not bring against him a reviling accusation, but said, 'The Lord rebuke you!'"—Jude 1:9*

Always Be Prepared for the Next Transition

Some day I won't be here, and somebody else will be here preaching. This will be their pulpit. And I might come and sit in that row and throw jellybeans at them or something, but that will be their role. But believe me, before they get here, the spiritual warfare will be intense and the training will be even more intense.

Always be prepared for the next transition. Stop going out with only half your armor on. You cause the leaders in the church to waste a lot of time when you didn't have your helmet on or because your shield wasn't up or because you didn't have your sword or your feet weren't shod. You didn't have on the belt of truth. We're spending too much time helping you recover from when you got the snot beat out of you because you didn't wear all the armor.

Essential Art and Skill of Spiritual Warfare

Anybody who serves as an Equipper will have warfare. When I equip people, I always teach them spiritual warfare. If you're just a coach or somebody on the sidelines, you won't have warfare. But when you step in and disciple somebody so their life becomes what it's supposed to be, you get attacked. That's why Jesus' disciples were killed.

There is an essential skill and art of warfare. I have a whole series of books by Sun Tzu, especially one called *The Art of War* that is required reading by every Marine entering the Marine Corps.

It's essential to learn the skill of war and it is essential to learn spiritual warfare. I believe many current intercessors on earth today are not attuned to the shift in warfare that has happened in the spiritual realm.

> *"And the angels who did not keep their proper domain, but left their own abode, He has reserved in everlasting chains under darkness for the judgment of the great day."—Jude 1:6*

In Revelation 20, the Bible says Satan was chained and put down in the bottomless pit. After Jesus comes back, he's put there for 1,000 years and then he's released and he pollutes the world again. He does all this stuff and the church has to rise up and be strong. There's is another whole unfolding of truth there.

> *"Then I saw an angel coming down from heaven, having the key to the bottomless pit and a great chain in his hand. He laid hold of the dragon, that serpent of old, who is the Devil and Satan, and bound him for a thousand years; and he cast him into the bottomless pit, and shut him up, and set a seal on him, so that he should deceive the nations no more till the thousand years were finished. But after these things he must be released for a little while."—Revelation 20:1-3*

Some of them were so violent, so horrible, that they had to be chained. They've been down in Hades and it says they will be released at a certain time, at an end of the age or in a time of judgment.

> *"For if God did not spare the angels who sinned, but cast them down to hell and delivered them into chains of darkness, to be reserved for judgment."*
> —2 Peter 2:4

I believe historically we're at the time where they have been loosed on the earth and they've never been on the earth in this capability of spiritual strength.

Remember, the archangel said to Satan, *"The Lord rebuke you!"* He didn't even feel he had the authority to rebuke Satan.

We need to understand that these demons on the earth today are beyond anything we've ever known. The average Christian is unprepared for the level of warfare that is actually going on, and it's going to increase.

16. Operating in the Gifts of the Spirit

"But one and the same Spirit works all these things,
distributing to each one individually as He wills."
—1 Corinthians 12:11

If you're called to be a pastor, there ought to be miracles, signs, and wonders following you. There should be discernment, if you're walking in eldership. If you're walking in deaconship, if you're walking in any of these roles that God has placed in the church, you should be operating in the gifts of the Spirit. If you're singing, you should be prophesying. If you're singing, you should have words of knowledge.

If you think you're anointed to sing and you have none of the gifts of God operating in your life, that's not the anointing. That's just your talent.

You're not anointed just because you say you are anointed. You're anointed when the nine gifts of the Spirit are part of the expression of that anointing.

Nine Gifts, Same Spirit—1 Corinthians 12:4-11

- *Same Spirit*—"There are diversities of gifts, but the same Spirit" *(verse 4).*
- *Same Lord*—"There are differences of ministries, but the same Lord" *(verse 5).*
- *Same God*—"And there are diversities of activities, but it is the same God who works all in all" *(verse 6).*
- *For the profit of all*—"But the manifestation of the Spirit is given to each one for the profit of all" *(verse 7):*

- *Word of wisdom through the Spirit*—"for to one is given the word of wisdom through the Spirit *(verse 8)*,
- *Word of knowledge through the same Spirit*—"to another the word of knowledge through the same Spirit" *(verse 9),*
- *Faith by the same Spirit*—"to another faith by the same Spirit" *(verse 9),*
- *Gifts of healings by the same Spirit*—"to another gifts of healings by the same Spirit" *(verse 9),*
- *Working of miracles*—"to another the working of miracles" *(verse 10),*
- *Prophecy*—"to another prophecy" *(verse 10).*
- *Discerning of spirits*—"to another discerning of spirits *(verse 10),*
- *Different kinds of tongues*—"to another different kinds of tongues" *(verse 10),*
- *Interpretation of tongues*—"to another the interpretation of tongues" *(verse 10).*
- *One and the same Spirit*—"But one and the same Spirit works all these things, distributing to each one individually as He wills" *(verse 11).*

You Need Your Own Encounter with the Holy Spirit

You may think you can borrow spirituality from people who can help you out with God. However, if you have not had an experience with the Holy Spirit yourself, what you borrow from others could become the reason you can't defeat the enemy.

We see a young man in the Bible who borrows an ax, and the axe head falls off.

> *"But as one was cutting down a tree, the iron ax head fell into the water; and he cried out and said, 'Alas, master! For it was borrowed.'"—2 Kings 6:5*

Equippers must be especially careful not to borrow. You can't borrow my prayer life. You can't borrow your mother's prayer life, you can't borrow your wife or your husband's relationship with God. That won't help you in the day of battle.

That's why the Lord said to Elijah in 1 Kings 17:3, "Go hide yourself" and in the next chapter He said, "Go show yourself to Ahab." Learn to listen and learn God's processes. If He told you to hide yourself first, then go show yourself, you would get mixed up if you decided to show yourself before you hid yourself.

Develop Your Own Ability to Hear God

David had weapons that were simple, but he was skilled in using them for the purposes of God. Here's the thing. God uses your talent, but He can't use your talent when your talent is greater than God in your eyes.

A good Equipper can develop your talent while also developing your ability to hear God. Then your natural talents are brought to bear in an environment of the supernatural.

Then there is the aspect of ability. You do need abilities that are borrowed from others. With the right Equipper, people learn to use their skills and merge their abilities with others under the anointing to bring glory to God together.

God did not use my grammar to make me who I am today. He didn't use that part of me. He used the part that I'm fearless. I jump out of the plane and THEN I ask, "Did you get the parachute?"

You need an anointing—a supernatural endowment from God—that shows you how to move fearlessly in the spirit.

17. Foundation of Character

"And when He had removed him, He raised up for them David as king, to whom also He gave testimony and said, 'I have found David the son of Jesse, a man after My own heart, who will do all My will.'"—Acts 13:22

Most school classrooms have at least one bad kid who occupies everyone's attention. Parents, teachers, anybody who has participated in education knows what I'm talking about.

I was that kid. I punched the principal in the stomach in the fifth grade, so you know I was a bad kid. I set the tone for the whole class. Even my classmates said, "If you get him out of here, we won't have to keep missing recess." Recess was a break time when all the kids went out to play, but my classmates were forced to sit in and miss recess because I got in a fight.

Bad Character

One kid can spoil the whole thing. The Bible says little foxes spoil the vines (Song of Solomon 2:15).

You need to get this. The greatest thing someone can ever do is sit you down if your character is weak. If you Remove someone who doesn't have the right character, you have saved their lives. You have saved them by not placing too much responsibility on them that could cause them to sin before God.

When you see somebody who has been set aside, you need to say, "Thank you, Jesus." If that had not been done in the church, you would have seen shipwrecks everywhere.

Troublemakers who think we ought to tolerate them are falling for the myth that the church is all about you.

They think the whole Bible was written to meet their needs. They say things like this: "I found the story that fits me."

Character, Not Gifting, Is the Foundation

Somebody once offered to replace me as pastor of Rock City Church. They knew how to preach so they said, "You're getting up in age, so you are probably ready to get somebody to come in and take over the church. You're getting old now."

Then they said to my wife and me, "The only condition is that we want you to leave the church. We want to take over the church, have the church, minister in the church, but we don't want you to sit there. We want you to leave."

I said, "Wait a minute. I want to be buried here. What are you talking about that you don't want me to be here?" That person had no concern with character. It was all about giftings.

The foundation of the Christian life is character, not giftings.

Pastors who encourage people to accept ministry assignments before they develop depth of character build churches that are personality-driven and based on talent.

Christians must be equipped with godly character for life and lasting ministry.

Senior leaders and pastors often place people in ministry based on giftings rather than integrity and character. All of us have done it and all of us can be guilty of this. We can find ourselves training people just because we like them or because they're available or because we need to fill a gap. But, in reality, we are moving away from the true qualities that should be guiding us—the integrity and character of that person whom we are equipping.

Equippers Correct Character Flaws and Lack of Integrity

People without integrity won't last long in ministry. That's why so many quit and fall away. Many were not equipped with proper doctrine or were placed in the wrong positions, but the real reason they failed was an Equipper who did not correct their character flaws and lack of integrity.

New churches where the pastor was not equipped and was sent out without a covering only last about three to five years. Often the problem is a failure of character. Not only the pastors fail but also the people they place in ministry under them. Pastors who are not properly equipped will promote singers and teachers based on talent. They prioritize giftings over integrity.

Don't Be Lenient with Those Whom God Disqualifies

Saul failed God as king of Israel because of character flaws. He was a rebel and a liar and he could not be trusted. God told Samuel to confront Saul with his disobedience:

> *"Behold, to obey is better than sacrifice. . . . Because you have rejected the word of the Lord, He also has rejected you from being king."—1 Samuel 15: 22, 23*

God was just and righteous in His action to Disqualify Saul as king, but Samuel had trouble accepting God's decision. The Lord had to rebuke Samuel, too, in order to maintain order. Then God sent Samuel to anoint David, who became a man after God's own heart.

"Now the Lord said to Samuel, 'How long will you mourn for Saul, seeing I have rejected him from reigning over Israel? Fill your horn with oil, and go; I am sending you to Jesse the Bethlehemite. For I have provided Myself a king among his sons.'"
—*1 Samuel 16:1*

God told Samuel, "I have found among Jesse's sons a king I can trust. I will set in place the one whom I decide." If church leaders got that right, they would avoid most of the issues that arise with rebels. When they are lenient with those whom God has Disqualified, they are being disobedient to God.

Character Qualities to Develop in Those Who Are Sent

Truthful. Speak the truth with neighbors, including pastors and leaders in your church, because you are members together. Even if you don't go around lying, do you sometimes lie when you say everything is good, everything is fine, yet you know that you are not walking the walk wherein you have been called?

> *"Therefore, putting away lying, 'Let each one of you speak truth with his neighbor,' for we are members of one another."*—*Ephesians 4:25*

Get angry for the right reasons, but never sin. The self-righteous go to church because they want peace, yet they will go out and be angry in the world when it suits them, even if they sin.

> *"Be angry, and do not sin."*—*Ephesians 4:26*

Never steal. *"Let him who stole steal no longer, but rather let him labor, working with his hands what is good, that he may have something to give him who has need."*
—*Ephesians 4:28*

Edify hearers with grace. *"Let no corrupt word proceed out of your mouth, but what is good for necessary*

edification, that it may impart grace to the hearers."
—Ephesians 4:29

Never grieve the Holy Ghost. *"And do not grieve the Holy Spirit of God, by whom you were sealed for the day of redemption. Let all bitterness, wrath, anger, clamor, and evil speaking be put away from you, with all malice. And be kind to one another, tenderhearted, forgiving one another, even as God in Christ forgave you."—Ephesians 4:29-32*

Confess your sins and forgive others. Forgiveness is not an automatic switch that I'm obligated to throw every time you mess up. You're responsible to confess your sin so that you can then be forgiven. You also need to forgive others.

> *"Confess your faults one to another, and pray one for another, that ye may be healed. The effectual fervent prayer of a righteous man availeth much."*
> *—James 5:16 KJV*

> *". . . and forgive us our sins, as we have forgiven those who sin against us."—Matthew 6:12 NLT*

Who Are You When No One's Around?

Character is who you really are when no one's around. Your character is exposed when you say something privately that you'd like to tell someone, but you won't tell them to their face.

God has to work on your character and who you are when no one's there. When you get the right Equipper, they will be working on your character. They will train you in God's school of character.

18. Patience to Pray and Wait on God

"But those who wait on the LORD
Shall renew their strength;
They shall mount up with wings like eagles,
They shall run and not be weary,
They shall walk and not faint."
—Isaiah 40:31

They that wait upon the Lord shall renew their strength. Every Christian needs to learn the value of waiting on God. He's never late. He's always on time. If you just wait on Him, then He has a chance to fix your character in the midst of your circumstances.

Some people are so impulsive that they always want dynamite answers. You need to slow down. Chill out. Take a break, because you might be running into God.

Be Patient So You Don't Elevate People Prematurely

It's imperative to understand that just because someone has a position, if they are still in training you cannot identify that as a firm position. After I bring in elders, I watch them for years. I don't appoint them, I bring them in to watch, to see.

I was on staff for nine years at Rock Church in Virginia Beach and everybody went out but me. My pastor tried to send my wife and me to churches four different times. We went, but then prophets would come in and say, "Yea, says the Lord, stop sending him."

So I made this statement. I don't want to go out until God has given me enough character to handle the big thing he wants me to do. I got offers from everybody. My response was, I'm just going to wait till the character fits the call, because when I go out I ain't coming back. And when I go out, I'm going to finish what I'm supposed to start.

You need to be mindful when you see people being trained and equipped in churches, such as Bible school students. When you see them in school, there is a tendency to elevate them to a level you should not do. You actually bring about more spiritual warfare than they can handle because they're not Sent. They are just helpers. They are assisting.

Be Faithful with Little

If you're not faithful with a little, you'll never have much. Ungodly ambition will drive you insane. You will be a fool because of ambition.

Learn the value of waiting on God. This is a principle if you're being equipped by a good Equipper.

> *"And he said to him, 'Well done, good servant; because you were faithful in a very little, have authority over ten cities.'"—Luke 19:17*

I never ask to go out to preach anywhere. Although I've had many invitations, I'm not anxious. I don't want anybody's seat but mine. I'm willing to wait on the Lord.

Section 4.

Those Who Are Sent, Removed, or Disqualified

19. The Sent

"I heard the voice of the Lord, saying:
"'Whom shall I send,
And who will go for Us?'
"Then I said, 'Here am I! Send me.'"
—Isaiah 6:8

Only one group of people is qualified to represent God and the senior leader—the Sent. They are Equipped in the church and sent out from the church. They multiply the best things about the church, by God's standards. My pastor used to say to me all the time, "Bart, in all the churches we plant, I ain't sending any failures."

Every Sent one starts out as a saint. The Sent are all saints. On the field, you either stay a saint or you become the Removed, like John Mark, so that you can grow up. If you fail, you become one of the Disqualified.

The Sent

Remember, there are three significant groups of people in Scripture—the Sent, the Removed, like John Mark, whom Paul removed from his ministry team on the field, and the Disqualified, like Judas.

The Removed and the Disqualified

People who are designated to be Removed or people who are Disqualified cannot be equipped and sent because they will end up being dividers. They will actually separate the church.

The Removed have their anointing out of whack.

The Disqualified speak against the leaders' anointing and in so doing they are actually speaking against the Holy Spirit who gave the leader the anointing. They are blaspheming God. They credit to the devil something that is of the Holy Spirit. The Disqualified twist the Bible to justify disloyalty.

You have to understand that this Bible is all connected. This book is not just floating out there. Every page, every word, is in synchronization with the others. Everything is connected.

Favor the Equipper, Not the Student Being Corrected

During the equipping process, a casual observer might see something being corrected in a person being equipped. Since it is happening within the church structure, and the church is like a family, a community, they have opinions about it.

However, remember that the Equipper is dealing with the preparation of a future leader, so you should respect the Equipper, not favor the student. When you see adjustments being made, keep quiet about your opinions. Learn not to put your mouth on it. Remember, the mouth is the place where demons operate. Demons come into the mouth and operate through the mouth.

Safeguard yourself from those pits of dishonor before you get trapped in them and don't know where you are.

Churches Need to Spend More Time Equipping Leaders

Senior pastors and apostolic leaders usually spend most of their time nurturing people and meeting needs rather than raising up and training new leaders who can become the Sent. The local church needs pastor/shepherds who take care of practical needs, but even more it needs its senior apostolic leaders equipping those who can become the Sent. They pluck out this one and that one to be trained for ministry, then work with them until they can be sent.

Apostolic leaders should focus 80 percent of their time on the 20 percent of the congregation who will do 80 percent of the ministry work. Jesus focused on His disciples. Then He sent them. Focus on the Sent.

Restoring the Alignment in the Sent

"Repent therefore and be converted, that your sins may be blotted out, so that times of refreshing may come from the presence of the Lord, and that He may send Jesus Christ, who was preached to you before, whom heaven must receive until the times of restoration of all things, which God has spoken by the mouth of all His holy prophets since the world began."
—Acts 3:19-21

I believe in the restoration of all things. I believe that by Christ's salvation God takes our rotten life and turns it into something good.

However, we have allowed the church to become just a place where you come to feel good when it should be the place where you are equipped for the work of the ministry.

If you have a home, husband, wife, kids, dog, cat, fish, you want everything in alignment. When things are in alignment, then you're thinking like a family. You're functioning alike. You're working together as one.

That's one of the things we are after as a church when we use Equippers.

When you get in alignment with Father, Son, and Holy Ghost, you get in alignment with God's will. That causes supernatural events to take place. Things begin to line up.

When the anointing of God is on you, it's all about the power of alignment. If you can get in alignment with those over you, if you get in alignment with the Holy Spirit, if you can get in alignment with God's Word, if you can get in alignment in your home, you can see the hand of God as never before.

How do you know His mighty power? When you're in alignment. There are divine alignments all through Scripture.

Take Time to Get in Alignment with the Holy Spirit

Equippers learn not to rush the process of equipping the Sent. The first thing an Equipper does is to get in alignment with the Holy Spirit. Then he begins to build some things that are important to be built. Strong commitments, foundations of loyalty, accomplishing the shared vision. Write the vision, making it plain.

When I'm raising up people and trying to work with them, that is the process that's going on in my head all the time.

Are they going to be loyal or disloyal? If they're disloyal, they get Removed and sometimes they get Disqualified.

David was looking to see if the men who came to him would be loyal. He said, *"If you have come peaceably to me to help me, my heart will be united with you"* (*1 Chronicles 12:17*).

Equippers Teach Loyalty to the Vision of the House

Building strong loyalty and laying the foundation are vital keys for accomplishing vision. The motives of those who serve in the inner circle must be filtered if you're going to be a person used as an Equipper. What does loyalty mean? It means being faithful and constant and true in relationships. This was David's team:

> *"Then some of the sons of Benjamin and Judah came to David at the stronghold. And David went out to meet them, and answered and said to them, 'If you have come peaceably to me to help me, my heart will be*

*united with you; but if to betray me to my enemies,
since there is no wrong in my hands, may the God of
our fathers look and bring judgment.' Then the Spirit
came upon Amasai, chief of the captains, and he said:*

> *"'We are yours, O David;
> We are on your side, O son of Jesse!
> Peace, peace to you,
> And peace to your helpers!
> For your God helps you.'"*

*"So David received them, and made them captains of
the troop."—1 Chronicles 12:16-18*

Don't Force Preachers to Equip Unprofitable People

God wants us to get this thing right.

We need to stop trying to equip people whom God has
not attached to us. We are wearing out preachers by expecting
them to equip everyone who comes their way. Preachers are
quitting all the time because they're trying to disciple and
equip people who are not profitable for the ministry. They may
be profitable later, but right now they can't be used.

Some May Fall, But I Will Remember the Lord!

Align yourself with God. Whatever happens on my
right hand or my left hand, as David said, 1,000 may fall at my
side and 10,000 at my right hand, but I will remember the
Lord!

> *"A thousand may fall at your side,
> And ten thousand at your right hand;
> But it shall not come near you."—Psalm 91:7*

20. The Removed

"But Paul insisted that they should not take with them the one who had departed from them in Pamphylia, and had not gone with them to the work."—Acts 15:38

People who have to be Removed are those who struggle in the equipping process and the spiritual warfare is so intense that they cannot be Sent. One example is John Mark, whom the Bible calls an assistant to Paul and Barnabas.

Paul and Barnabas Were Sent, But John Just Came Along

In Acts13:1, the Bible mentions several leaders in the church at Antioch. Then it says in Acts 13:2 that the Holy Spirit said to separate Barnabas and Saul (Paul) to be Sent. The Bible also notes that John Mark came along as an assistant.

> *"Now in the church that was at Antioch there were certain prophets and teachers: Barnabas, Simeon who was called Niger, Lucius of Cyrene, Manaen who had been brought up with Herod the tetrarch, and Saul. As they ministered to the Lord and fasted, the Holy Spirit said, 'Now separate to Me Barnabas and Saul for the work to which I have called them.'"—Acts 13:1-2*

> *"Then, having fasted and prayed, and laid hands on them, they sent them away. So, being sent out by the Holy Spirit, they went down to Seleucia, and from there they sailed to Cyprus. And when they arrived in Salamis, they preached the word of God in the synagogues of the Jews.*

> *"They also had John as their assistant."—Acts 13:3-5*

Notice this. Paul and Barnabas were Sent, but John Mark was only their assistant (NLT) or helper (NIV). John

Mark was not *Sent* by the Holy Spirit. Barnabas just took him along.

Sent, but Something Was Out of Alignment

Soon they ran into a problem in Paphos—a sorcerer. The church at Antioch had just laid hands on Barnabas and Saul to be Sent, but now they were already in deep spiritual warfare. Something was out of alignment.

> *"Now when they had gone through the island to Paphos, they found a certain sorcerer, a false prophet, a Jew whose name was Bar-Jesus who was with the proconsul, Sergius Paulus, an intelligent man. This man called for Barnabas and Saul and sought to hear the word of God."—Acts 13:6-7*

The Greeks were the scholars of the day. They said, "Let's bring them in (Paul and Barnabas) and listen to them." This is typical of the Greeks. They were searchers after intelligence.

So here are Paul and Barnabas on their first mission and they're hardly out the door when somebody is in their midst trying to turn a leader away from faith in Jesus.

> *"Sergius Paulus, an intelligent man. This man called for Barnabas and Saul and sought to hear the word of God.*
>
> *"But Elymas the sorcerer (for so his name is translated) withstood them, seeking to turn the proconsul away from the faith.*
>
> *"Then Saul, who also is called Paul, filled with the Holy Spirit, looked intently at him and said, 'O full of all deceit and all fraud, you son of the devil, you enemy of all righteousness, will you not cease perverting the straight ways of the Lord? And now, indeed, the hand of the Lord is upon you, and you shall be blind, not seeing the sun for a time.'*

"And immediately a dark mist fell on him, and he went around seeking someone to lead him by the hand. Then the proconsul believed, when he saw what had been done, being astonished at the teaching of the Lord.

"Now when Paul and his party set sail from Paphos, they came to Perga in Pamphylia; and John, departing from them, returned to Jerusalem."—Acts 13:6-13

Paul is in it now. He has activated the gift of discernment. He is brand new at this. He calls the guy a devil. *"You son of the devil."* He is dealing with him. Paul knew about blindness from personal experience. He prophesies and speaks to the false prophet, "You're going to be blind."

Barnabas Disagreed with Paul's Decision to Remove John

Paul and Barnabas traveled together and had many missionary adventures. They reached one end of the process and now they were going back to sail through all the cities and see how everyone was doing.

"Then after some days Paul said to Barnabas, 'Let us now go back and visit our brethren in every city where we have preached the word of the Lord, and see how they are doing.'"—Acts 15:36

However, it seemed that something was still out of alignment. In Acts 15, the contention between them came out in the open. It centered on John Mark, who had not been Sent, as they had. Paul decided John Mark should be Removed, but Barnabas disagreed. Notice that Barnabas was determined, not led of the Lord.

"Now Barnabas was determined to take with them John called Mark."—Acts 15:37

You have to stop and ponder the divisive effect of John Mark and the reason Paul had to Remove him. Paul said, "He is not going with us."

Paul is the guy who had prophesied over someone who went blind. You might think his ministry associate, Barnabas, would let Paul have a lead voice in determining which causes should result in someone being Removed.

Removed for Cause

In law, someone is Removed *"for cause"* when the capability of that person for a particular function is challenged. Paul was challenging John Mark's capability for the mission field. He didn't want to take someone who had departed from them. John Mark had deserted them, and Paul believed that was ample cause to Remove him, not Send him, *for cause.*

Yet Barnabas took the side of John Mark, and Paul and Barnabas separated over this contention.

> *"But Paul insisted that they should not take with them the one who had departed from them in Pamphylia, and had not gone with them to the work. Then the contention became so sharp that they parted from one another."—Acts 15:38-39*

John Mark Was Removed, Not Permanently Disqualified

The Removed can be restored if they change. This is the key. After he was removed, John Mark apparently learned an important lesson. After he recovered from the shock, he must have had the good sense to do some self-examination and get his act together so he could be used.

Later in the story, you see that Paul calls for John Mark to return. It's after maybe 10, 15, 20 years, so maybe some maturity happened, maybe some things took place that woke up John Mark so that he had more stability in his life.

Paul sends word to Timothy that he can use John Mark now. He has heard that John Mark is doing much better and he writes, "Bring him to me."

"Be diligent to come to me quickly; for Demas has forsaken me, having loved this present world, and has departed for Thessalonica—Crescens for Galatia, Titus for Dalmatia. Only Luke is with me. Get Mark and bring him with you, for he is useful to me for ministry."—2 Timothy 4:9-11

Note the difference. John Mark, once Removed, is coming back, but Demas has been Disqualified and is never coming back.

John Mark's Removal, Paul's Unity with Silas and Timothy

After John Mark left with Barnabas, we see Paul choosing Silas as his companion.

". . . but Paul chose Silas and departed, being commended by the brethren to the grace of God. And he went through Syria and Cilicia, strengthening the churches."—Acts 15:40-41

Paul and Silas ended up in jail together. They had many dangerous adventures, but they were compatible.

Compatibility is a key to ministry success. The church is weak when there's no unity of leadership.

When Paul had unity with his companions, he could strengthen the church.

Timothy Became a Son

God often takes people away when He's setting things in order. Someone gets Removed who is abusing this process of equipping. John Mark was Removed from Paul because they were not able to work together, and Paul was the leader.

Then in Acts 16, God sends a young man to Paul named Timothy. His mother loved the Lord and his grandmother loved the Lord. What does Paul do? He circumcises Timothy. Hi, welcome to the ministry!

Paul saw something in Timothy that he had not seen in John Mark. He knew he should do the circumcision because Timothy's father was Greek and had brought in the Gentile position. Paul knew if he was going to use Timothy, he had to bring him under the covenant as a Jew, which required circumcision. Timothy was willing to do it, and he ain't no little kid. So Paul takes this guy and circumcises him.

The story unfolds in First and Second Timothy that Timothy was a son. Paul calls him "my son, my beloved son." Paul adopted this guy as a son, and that's important.

Sometimes God has to remove somebody so that He can move the right person into the line. God says He raises up one and He sets down another. He holds kings in the palm of his hands.

You need to know that God is the one who sets people in the body as it pleases Him. You must get that. When you keep interfering, you get nothing but constipation.

"But God is the judge: he putteth down one, and setteth up another."—Psalm 75:7 KJV

Sometimes a Son Is Revealed After Someone Else Is Removed

John Mark is Removed, then God sends Timothy. All of a sudden, this young Timothy appears. He was the same Timothy who had the largest mega church in all of Bible history. He had a massive church. Timothy's mother and grandmother had prayed over him, prophesied to him, and laid hands on him.

Paul refers to Timothy as his son—*"my beloved and faithful son in the Lord" (1 Corinthians 4:17)*. This was a sonship—father and son.

Paul said, "You have many instructors but not many fathers."

*"For though you might have ten thousand instructors in Christ, yet **you do not have many fathers**; for in Christ Jesus I have begotten you through the gospel."—1 Corinthians 4:15*

*"This charge I commit to you, **son Timothy**, according to the prophecies previously made concerning you, that by them you may wage the good warfare."*
—1 Timothy 1:18

Notice how Paul has moved from just speaking of Timothy by name to also speaking of him as a son.

Reasons for Removal

One of the greatest mistakes I have made in ministry is to bring people on and bring people around who were not supposed to be there. I tried to work with them, but they were not qualified. Here are several reasons why someone should be Removed.

Some Reasons for Removal

1. Removed because it was not "a good idea" after all

2. Removed because leader compromised to fill a need

3. Removed because you just can't work with them

4. Removed because they are not trustworthy

5. Removed because they bring disruption

6. Removed because they live a double standard

7. Removed for murmuring

---

1. Removed because it was not "a good idea" after

The prophets and teachers at Antioch had se⌐
Barnabas and Saul, who was also known as Paul.

> *"Then having fasted and prayed and laid hands on*
> *them. So, being sent out by the Holy Spirit."*
> *—Acts 13:3-4*

I believe strongly in the laying on of hands. It is an impartation. We need to be careful that we don't lay hands on everybody just because it sounds good. Paul warns about laying on hands too quickly, lest they become conceited and fall into the same condemnation incurred by the devil.

> *Do not lay hands on anyone hastily, nor share in other*
> *people's sins; keep yourself pure."—1 Timothy 5:22*

John Mark was not included in the laying on of hands and was not Sent. Barnabas made the decision to bring John Mark along because he was a friend. John Mark wasn't Sent. He wasn't called. He wasn't qualified. Barnabas just thought it was a good idea to bring him along.

Paul and Barnabas were Sent by the Holy Spirit, not because it was a good idea. They were not sent because of a need, even though there must have been needs in that area. You feed people because of a need but you don't Send people in ministry because of a need. You need to hear from the Holy Spirit.

> *"So being sent out by the Holy Spirit they went down to*
> *Seleucia and from there they sailed to Cyprus. And*
> *when they arrived in Salamis they preached the word*
> *of God in the synagogues of the Jews. They also had*
> *John as their assistant."—Acts 13:4-5*

John was just an assistant. He was not Sent. They brought him along and it didn't work out. That's a good lesson.

. Removed because leader compromised to fill a need

I always warn people to be careful not to fill a need with a person just because you have a need. That is done in business, and I have done that in ministry, but the results are never good.

God is ultimately the One who fulfills our needs, so we don't have to compromise.

> *"And my God shall supply all your need according to His riches in glory by Christ Jesus."—Philippians 4:19*

3. Removed because you just can't work with them

Paul could not work with John Mark. Paul's personality, Paul's anointing, who he was, there was some friction there and finally Paul said that Mark had to go. He sent John Mark away. He was Removed. Barnabas took him and they separated because Paul couldn't work with him.

I want you to know something. There are many, many times when you are training people in church and you find you just can't work with certain people. You know that in your life there are certain people in your family you don't get along with. There are certain people in your business you don't get along with. That doesn't mean that one's right and the other's wrong. It just means when you're doing something that God told you to do you have to stay within the confines of what God said.

4. Removed because they are not trustworthy

The Bible says John Mark left them. He abandoned the ministry. He walked away from the things of God.

> **Paul said, "No way! I don't want him with us because I can't trust him in the day of a battle."**

> *"But Paul insisted that they should not take with them the one who had departed from them in Pamphylia, and had not gone with them to the work."—Acts 15:38*

5. Removed because they bring disruption

When some people are around, there seems to be a lot of disruption. You can't seem to stop all the craziness that goes on. Devilish attacks start to happen. When I am unable to train somebody like that, I don't want them to stay around. I don't want them to give a prophetic word and cause even more confusion.

When I am equipping the saints, I want an atmosphere of agreement. How can two walk together except they agree!

"Can two walk together, unless they are agreed?"
—Amos 3:3

6. Removed because they live a double standard

Many factors have to be right before you can be successful in this process of equipping. When somebody is living a double standard, they're not living for God, and you can't equip them. You have to put them away, Remove them, put them aside. You have to move them out so that they don't get destroyed. If you elevate them and send them out, the devil will beat the hell out of them.

7. Removed for murmuring

When God deals with people, some get removed and others who can't handle the removal process become Disqualified because they have the wrong attitude toward justice.

The apostles and prophets decide who needs to be removed and who is Disqualified. That is a vital operation.

"Then Miriam and Aaron spoke against Moses . . . And the Lord heard it."—Numbers 12:1-2

The Lord called out Aaron and Miriam for their rebellion against the leader, Moses, and they experienced the judgment of God.

"So the anger of the Lord was aroused against them, and He departed. And when the cloud departed from above the tabernacle, suddenly Miriam became leprous, as white as snow."—Numbers 12:9-10

Don't Criticize Equippers When They Remove Someone

When you see somebody getting shuffled out, leave it alone. Keep your mouth off it. Let God deal with them. Unless you have the power to deliver them and bring them into the Kingdom on your own, don't touch it. Watch God bring something good out of it.

When John Mark is removed, Timothy comes in and he is a powerful addition. Timothy became a son. Timothy became profitable for everything Paul was now doing. But Paul did not get Timothy until he got rid of John Mark.

Don't be afraid to make the right choices

We need Equippers who are not afraid to make the right choices. Sometimes people occupy a spot that someone else is supposed to occupy. You see that in sports. It happens in business. It happens in every field where there are people. There are politicians who try to do something good, but they are not necessarily the ones God wants in office.

John Mark went on the mission because he was invited, and so eventually he was Removed. But Timothy was Sent.

The Removed have the potential to return. Years later the Bible tells us that John Mark rejoined Paul. Paul asked for him because I believe John Mark had matured and came to a place where God could really use him and use him in a great way. It took a few years, but it was good enough for Paul to make his adjustments and for John Mark to get his act together and go.

Don't interfere with the Lord's discipline

When leaders are fulfilling their responsibility concerning the discipline of certain people, you need to back off. Don't put your hand on it, because God might deal with you like he dealt with Miriam. All of a sudden, you're going to find yourself with leprosy. Numbers 16 relates the account of the rebellion of Korah and other leaders who rose up against Moses and Aaron.

> *"Now it came to pass, as he finished speaking all these words, that the ground split apart under them, and the earth opened its mouth and swallowed them up, with their households and all the men with Korah, with all their goods."—Numbers 16:31-32*

If you murmur against your leader, you, too, could get removed or disqualified or even swallowed up by the earth.

Misdirected saints see a leader who is being discipled by the pastor but don't like the process. They would not have trained a leader that way. They would have softened it and compromised standards when the see the trainee's sins so they challenge the pastor. When they see the process not going their way, they murmur to others. They say, "Oh, the pastor is wrong."

But they are wrong. The pastor is not the one who is being equipped and is not ready to be Sent. The pastor is the Equipper. He is the trainer, and the trainee is not fully trained yet. Maybe he has to be Removed for a time, or maybe he is responding so poorly to the equipping process that he is moving close to the line of being Disqualified. If the trainee is Disqualified, that means he will never get in the ministry, ever.

Confrontation in the congregation

At one Thursday night service I went over to a girl and said, "If you go to bed with another man in this church, I'm going to physically throw you out of the church."

The whole church gasped. One woman said, "I can't believe you did that. You embarrassed that woman. I'm offended."

I said, "Well, I am sorry that you're offended but that didn't change what I had to do."

The next morning the girl's picture was on the cover of the *Baltimore Sun.* The article said that she had molested 10 little boys as a music director. God showed me the problem. I exposed it publicly and put my finger on the girl. When I did what God said, those without spiritual understanding said, "Oh my God!"

If she were your child, you would have been grateful. You would have come to me and said, "I want to shake your hand, pastor. You have shown my daughter her sins."

Pastor's Authority Over Murmurers

Most pastors and leaders don't know their own authority under God to make decisions, so they become discouraged by the murmuring among the members. Pastor should walk in their authority to rescue those on the pathway to becoming Disqualified by Removing them before it is too late.

Those who murmur at the Equippers are not only out of order. They are also preventing those who have the potential to be Sent from receiving the only move that can save them— the pastor's willingness to remove them for further development.

In 1 Timothy 1:20, Paul made a leadership decision to set aside Hymenaeus and Alexander so they could learn the dangers of blasphemy before they became disqualified. He even said that he turned them over to Satan for a time. Their rebellion was the cause of their loss.

Good solid biblical teaching delivers you from misconceptions. Paul made the best decision to help them.

21. The Disqualified

Jesus said, "Assuredly, I say to you, all sins will be forgiven the sons of men, and whatever blasphemies they may utter; but he who blasphemes against the Holy Spirit never has forgiveness, but is subject to eternal condemnation."—Mark 3:28-29

So there are the Sent, then there are the Removed, and finally there are the Disqualified. Jesus said that some people will be permanently disqualified—with no redress—if they commit blasphemy against the Holy Spirit. Never lie to the Holy Ghost or deny that God did something by the Holy Ghost.

---

10 Reasons You Could Be Disqualified

1. Disqualified by lying to the Holy Ghost—Ananias and Sapphira

2. Disqualified by character defects—Saul

3. Disqualified by rebellion, stubborn, independent attitude, refusal to change—Judas, Lucifer

4. Disqualified by a wounded spirit and from imagined slights

5. Disqualified by judgmentalism and fault-finding

6. Disqualified by ambitious personal agendas

7. Disqualified by resistance to God's Word—Alexander the Coppersmith

8. Disqualified by demon possession—Elymas

9. Disqualified for preeminence of music over the Word

10. Disqualified for murmuring against leaders

11. Disqualified for loving to be praised

When the Disqualified are in control, that's how wolves can come in. That's why churches come undone and people are not coming back to church. Pastors have all kinds of goofy stuff going on because they allow anybody to get in their pulpit. They even allow people to lead their worship who are demon-possessed, full of lust, and have sex with the same sex.

> *"And anyone who speaks a word against the Son of Man, it will be forgiven him; but to him who blasphemes against the Holy Spirit, it will not be forgiven."—Luke 12:10*

1. Disqualified by lying to the Holy Ghost—Ananias and Sapphira

> *"But a certain man named Ananias, with Sapphira his wife, sold a possession. And he kept back part of the proceeds, his wife also being aware of it, and brought a certain part and laid it at the apostles' feet.*

> *"But Peter said, 'Ananias, why has Satan filled your heart to lie to the Holy Spirit and keep back part of the price of the land for yourself? While it remained, was it not your own? And after it was sold, was it not in your own control? Why have you conceived this thing in your heart? You have not lied to men but to God.'*

> *"Then Ananias, hearing these words, fell down and breathed his last. So great fear came upon all those who heard these things. And the young men arose and wrapped him up, carried him out, and buried him."—Acts 5:1-6*

Ananias and Sapphira were potential candidates for being equipped and Sent. They were already so committed that they were willing to take their land and sell it. I believe they got saved the first day Peter went out and preached when 3,000 got saved.

The Bible says they had all things in common. They sold their land and gave it to the Apostles for the work of the ministry. But here's a perfect example of somebody who gets disqualified. They didn't have good character. They lied to the Holy Ghost. You can tell me anything you want to tell me otherwise, but I know that people do it all the time. They say, "I did that, I got that done, I'm doing that." But they are lying. You can lie to me but I'm going to tell you what, when you start lying to the Holy Ghost, you're in trouble.

2. Disqualified by character defects—Saul

"But the LORD said to Samuel, 'Do not look at his appearance or at his physical stature, because I have refused him. For the LORD does not see as man sees; for man looks at the outward appearance, but the LORD looks at the heart.'"—1 Samuel 17:7

Even if people have skills and qualifications, sometimes you get the sense that something is still not right.

Character bend. The term I use when I feel something is not right is to say there is a bend in their character. They have a bend in their life, in their character. Here's what I mean.

When you have a wheel with a bend in it, the wheel won't roll right. Your car shakes, your steering wheel shakes. It's out of alignment. We're made of metal. We're like iron, and when our iron gets bent, unless we allow the heat to be applied, we can't ever get it straight.

I prophesied to a young man who had been in this church since he was a little boy. I said to him, "You are bent and so is your family, your sisters and brothers." They all were in trouble. They were in debt. They were under investigation, things like that.

If your metal is bent, everything you do is crooked. This kid's father ripped off his own business. The whole family was bent, and unless you get that thing straight, everything you've been doing is going to tilt unless heat is applied to your metal.

I've had to deal with so many people who have great ambitions and people who even have great talents, but their metal is bent. What caused the metal to bend?

When God Sets People Down, Agree with God

This is my prophecy. I hear the Lord say, Put away your towels. Put away your towels of mourning. Stop weeping for the Saul that God removed and listen for the appointment of God's anointing. God is going to anoint a new generation. He's going to anoint a new people. He's going to call some people.

In church, I watch people who used to be happy going around crying, mourning, and weeping because they see a decision that God made and they don't like the way *God* made it! We need to learn to let God set people down and raise people up and not attack His decisions with our judgmental attitudes. Just see things, accept them, and say, "Amen! God is in charge!"

When the Lord told Samuel that Saul was Disqualified, Samuel mourned for Saul instead of moving out in agreement with God. Samuel had an attitude because he liked Saul. But God had said, "I reject Saul from his position of reigning over Israel."

God knows everything. We don't. We need to understand that God deals with things from His position of absolute wisdom and authority. He does not suffer from personal attitudes. He's not over there whining. He's not having an attitude.

"But the LORD said, 'Take a heifer'" (1 Samuel 16:2). A prophet like Samuel knew that when he had oil in the horn, he was getting ready to go do some anointing. God stopped Samuel from mourning about a decision he didn't like, something that God did, because it was time to anoint someone else.

Notice how God shakes Samuel out of his bad attitude and puts him back in the frontlines of ministry. In other words, God says to Samuel, "Get over it! Get over this thing!" God says, "I rejected Saul. You got a problem with Me?" Then He says, "Get the horn, because I'm going to put you in ministry again."

God is just so locked in on what He's going to do that He doesn't even offer Samuel a towel to cry with. He just says, "Get a bucket of oil and get an old cow. We're going to have a party, boy. And say to Jesse, 'I have come to sacrifice to the Lord.' Then invite Jesse to the sacrifice and I'll show you what you should do."

Notice this. All equipping of the saints must be associated with sacrifice. If they're not willing to sacrifice, you can't use them!

Samuel did what the Lord said

"Now the Lord said to Samuel, 'How long will you mourn for Saul, seeing I have rejected him from reigning over Israel? Fill your horn with oil, and go; I am sending you to Jesse the Bethlehemite. For I have provided Myself a king among his sons.'

"And Samuel said, 'How can I go? If Saul hears it, he will kill me.'

"But the Lord said, 'Take a heifer with you, and say, "I have come to sacrifice to the Lord." Then invite Jesse to the sacrifice, and I will show you what you shall do; you shall anoint for Me the one I name to you.'

"So Samuel did what the Lord said, and went to Bethlehem. And the elders of the town trembled at his coming, and said, 'Do you come peaceably?'

"And he said, 'Peaceably; I have come to sacrifice to the Lord. Sanctify yourselves, and come with me to the sacrifice.' Then he consecrated Jesse and his sons, and invited them to the sacrifice.

"So it was, when they came, that he looked at Eliab and said, 'Surely the Lord's anointed is before Him!'

"But the Lord said to Samuel, 'Do not look at his appearance or at his physical stature, because I have refused him. For the Lord does not see as man sees; for man looks at the outward appearance, but the Lord looks at the heart.'

"So Jesse called Abinadab, and made him pass before Samuel. And he said, 'Neither has the Lord chosen this one.' Then Jesse made Shammah pass by. And he said, 'Neither has the Lord chosen this one.' Thus Jesse made seven of his sons pass before Samuel. And Samuel said to Jesse, 'The Lord has not chosen these.' And Samuel said to Jesse, 'Are all the young men here?' Then he said, 'There remains yet the youngest, and there he is, keeping the sheep.'

"And Samuel said to Jesse, 'Send and bring him. For we will not sit down till he comes here.' So he sent and brought him in. Now he was ruddy, with bright eyes, and good-looking. And the Lord said, 'Arise, anoint him; for this is the one!' Then Samuel took the horn of oil and anointed him in the midst of his brothers; and the Spirit of the Lord came upon David from that day forward. So Samuel arose and went to Ramah."—1 Samuel 16:1-13

Samuel went from mourning to anointing

God says, "Fill your horn with oil!" In other words, He says to Samuel, "Get the oil out, Son. Pour it in there. Fill that thing up. You know what I am going to do."

God said to Samuel, "Listen to me. I don't have time to raise up failures. You don't have time to argue with God. Get the horn out, Samuel, we're going to do business."

Samuel says, "OK, God. All right, I'm over it. I got that off me, I feel good."

God says, "Now, go. I'm sending you to Jesse the Bethlehemite."

Samuel says, "I know Jesse's got a bunch of boys. Well, I feel this anointing equipping is coming on! I'm equipping some guys." Samuel's thinking in his head "For I have provided myself a king among his sons. Wait a minute. Jesse's got six or seven sons and I only have to choose one of them. Well, it's not going to be hard because the boys are good looking, they're tall, they're handsome, and all that."

3. Disqualified by rebellious, stubborn, independent attitude, refusal to change—Judas, Lucifer

Jesus prayed about His disciples, "While I was with them in the world, I kept them in Your name. Those whom You gave Me I have kept; and none of them is lost except the son of perdition, that the Scripture might be fulfilled."—John 17:12

Judas, the son of perdition, was an independent person who wanted things his own way. Independent people are not team players. They are stubborn, addicted to their own way, and refuse to change. They are like a two-year-old, always deciding to do it their way. "I'll do it my way."

4. Disqualified by a wounded spirit and imagined slights

"A brother offended is harder to win than a strong city, And contentions are like the bars of a castle."—Proverbs 18:19

Some people develop a wounded spirit as a defense to justify incorrect positions. They distrust others' authority but want to exercise authority at the same time. When things are not done the way they think they should be done, they get offended.

Kind is attracted to kind and kind produces kind. A person who is always discontented unless they have created something themselves is also easily offended. They always pick up offense from others. When you're an Equipper working with them, you know that unless they change, they will always attract the same kind of people who love themselves. If they become a leader, their leadership will produce people like that who don't represent God.

5. Disqualified by judgmentalism and fault-finding

Equippers must be wary of accepting advice from judgmental people. They cannot be trusted.

If I'm discussing personnel issues with a fellow Equipper and they give me judgmental advice, I will immediately correct them. While I was expecting insight on how to help someone, the person I'm asking used it as a judgmental moment. That response triggers an alert in me that this person is bent metal. I need to get this straight.

The Bible says that Jesus didn't trust any man.

"Now when He was in Jerusalem at the Passover, during the feast, many believed in His name when they saw the signs which He did. But Jesus did not commit Himself to them, because He knew all men, and had no need that anyone should testify of man, for He knew what was in man."—John 2:23-25

Jesus knew what was in their hearts. Jesus knew that he couldn't trust them yet because they had not been converted. Remember that Jesus said to Peter, "Peter, when you've been converted" then you will lead many.

6. Disqualified by their ambitious personal agendas

This is one of the top areas that move a person down the path to Disqualification and the Equipper has to learn to spot this. They are overly ambitious with their personal agendas, and they can never fully commit to any other vision but their own. That's where the Equipper's discipleship comes in, when he has a conversation with a person who's not happy because he just learned that he could not have what he wanted. They are always pushing back and pushing against. I'm not talking about having an opinion. I'm not talking about having a creative suggestion. I'm talking about when it's just a natural thing for you when your first words are self-centered—"Let me tell you what I . . ."

Know-it-all, refusing to be taught

Over many years I've watched people come in and say, "I'm called to this," and then they have left. They're gone. You're trying to talk to them and you're trying to bring them into a place of character change and life change, but they are stuck in their attitudes. You can't do anything with those people. I would rather have somebody come and say, "I don't know how to do anything." I can teach that person something, but not when they come in and say, "I know everything. I got this down. I got everything down."

Unwilling to die to self-centered personal agendas

Equipping is a process of transformation Unless during the process those being equipped become willing to die to their own personal agendas, they will not achieve all that God wants. This process requires sacrifice. If you don't die to yourself, you'll bring too much of yourself into the thing that God wants to do and God will have to Disqualify you, not just Remove you.

7. Disqualified by resisting God's Word—Alexander the Coppersmith

When you live in violation of God's Word, you do not see the blessing of God because you're violating a truth. I could tithe to my own business and never see the fruit of my tithe because the Word doesn't tell you to do that. You can do a lot of good things but good things and God's things are not always the same.

"Alexander the coppersmith did me much harm. May the Lord repay him according to his works."—2 Timothy 4:14

Alexander the coppersmith would have been a very wealthy man. When you were a coppersmith, you were a very talented, on-demand guy. Idols were made of copper. Jewelry was made of copper. Even what we call silverware was made of copper. So, Alexander was supporting things and had some sense of responsibility.

A coppersmith was skilled in trades. He was a businessman who had money and he was probably doing some things that were not right that were hurting the ministry and hurting Paul and his effectiveness. Paul is upset because Alexander did him much harm. In 2 Timothy 4:15 he says, *"You also must beware of him, for he has greatly resisted our words."*

In other words, I can imagine Paul saying, "Listen to me, Alexander. You have to give that thing up. You have to get out of that business." Maybe he was into the pornography business. I don't know. But Paul said, "You have to give up that business and get back and listen to my words." But Alexander resisted. That's the Disqualified. That's the rebel who gets Disqualified.

In other words, Paul is saying, "Alexander rebelled. He wouldn't listen. He didn't listen to what I said, and I have rejected him."

There are those in church who will be Disqualified because they resist the Word of the Lord. The preached word, the prophetic word—they resist the Word. They don't want to hear the word. That's why so many don't come when I'm out of town. They don't want to have to hear the word. When I am in town, they think I will see them, so they come for show. You know, that's just as empty as you want to be. If you come to church so somebody can see you, 99 percent of the time I won't even see you, so don't think of yourself as so great.

8. Disqualified by Demon Possession—Elymas

"But Elymas the sorcerer (for so his name is translated) withstood them, seeking to turn the proconsul away from the faith."—Acts 13:8

This sorcerer Elymas was a phony. He was playing games, *"seeking to turn the proconsul away from the faith."* This man Elymas the sorcerer is not solid in his walk, yet he is pulling on the proconsul, trying to drag him away.

> *"Then Saul, who also is called Paul, filled with the Holy Spirit, looked intently at him and said, "O full of all deceit and all fraud, you son of the devil, you enemy of all righteousness, will you not cease perverting the straight ways of the Lord? And now, indeed, the hand of the Lord is upon you, and you shall be blind, not seeing the sun for a time."—Acts 13:9-11*

Man, I like the Bible's description! You look intently in somebody's eyes and straighten up and tell them, *"What you just said is not God."* Now that's some heavy prophecy.

I believe we're moving in days like that when God's servants will be bold and not afraid to operate with that kind of authority. The power of God is strong enough, but too many of God's servants are afraid to speak the truth.

In Acts 13:10, Paul rebuked Elymas the magician for opposing the Gospel, calling him a son of the devil. If a modern-day church preacher was to call one of the saints of God a son of the devil there'd be a revolt. People would say, "I'm not going to that church. I'm going somewhere that they tell me how much they love me."

In 2 Corinthians 4:4, Paul speaks of Satan as the god of this world who has blinded the minds of the unbelieving that they might not see the light of the Gospel of the Glory of Christ.

9. Disqualified for preeminence of music over the Word

People are praying that the church comes back from the all-music church! When you build a church on music, you're going to have a problem. That's why Hillsong is coming undone because they built it on the wrong stuff. You can't build it on something other than the Bible. There's a cleaning coming on!

10. Disqualified for murmuring against leaders

Have you ever been around somebody who softly says something negative to you that they only want you to hear? They say it under their breath. That's murmuring. If you do it in church, you risk the judgment of God.

Don't interfere with the training of a man or woman of God who may some day need what they are learning to save their own and others' lives. Don't try to intercept the correction of those who are being equipped. When you are not in the position to do the equipping, you have no right to murmur against the Equipper.

What's the problem in the church? We don't like God's appointments. We criticize with our mouth who God sets in the body and we criticize the leadership that God puts in because we don't like that one and we like this one instead.

Miriam murmured against Moses and got leprosy

Remember the story of Moses. The Bible says that Miriam and her little group complained to one another and she and Aaron said to Moses, "We could do just as good a job as you can do."

And the Lord said, "Moses, step aside."

Then God gave Miriam leprosy for murmuring against her leader. She remembered the lesson for the rest of her life.

Leprosy was the penalty for murmuring against Moses. Don't murmur.

Elders murmured against a pastor, and they died

In the church where we grew up, reality was always present. One time a Canadian pastor named Winston Nunes came to preach. He had a little bow tie and looked like a nerd, like Mr. Popcorn guy. Pastor Nunes had a Bible school of about 100 students and he said once he looked up and saw angels of heaven sitting around inside the rafters of the Bible school.

Pastor Nunes once spoke at a church and said, "You have seven elders. All seven elders please stand up." They stood and he said, "By this time next year, each of you will be dead because you murmured." My pastor, John Gimenez, was able to verify later that all seven of them had dropped dead.

11. Disqualified for loving to be praised

My friend Jim Bakker went to church with my wife and me. His kids were in nursery with my kids. I remember him saying to the people, "Stop making me bigger than God or you will kill me. Our God will remove me." And God Removed him. God could have Disqualified him, but Jim repented. He said, "I was wrong."

Pastors are not popularity contestants.

I don't want people to like me before they respect me. If respecting me you end up liking me, good for you.

There are people you like but God will deliberately keep them out of your presence because you would choose them to be above what He wanted them to be. That's why I do my best to keep people from liking me too much because they will sign my death warrant.

We have preachers who see themselves as popularity contestants. They want people to like them. God doesn't do things that way. I want to help pastors to grow up and get over coddling people to the point where they are not effective.

I am mentoring a kid and I'm being straight with him. I'm talking to him about issues in the city and region and I'm helping him. And because of this straight talk this kid is getting hungry and this kid led prayer and he brought the house down. When I first started meeting with him, he wouldn't even pray. I mean, he would whisper a prayer. Now he's praying out loud.

People should be trembling before the prophets[2]

"So Samuel did what the LORD said, and went to Bethlehem. And the elders of the town trembled at his coming, and said, "Do you come peaceably?"—1 Samuel 16:4

Isn't that good? We don't tremble today when the prophets come. We start pushing and shoving and trying to get in to get the best seat so we can get a word because we know the prophets are only going to say something good.

"And the elders of the town trembled at his coming and said, 'Do you come peaceably?'" In other words, when the prophet came to town you would be afraid with the fear of God. You would be trembling with apprehension as you asked him, "Are you coming here peacefully, man? Or are you coming here just to mess up everything?"

Samuel didn't say, "I'm coming to mess up everything. I'm going to get one of these boys out of the family of Jesse and anoint him the next king." He said only, "I have come peaceably. I have come to sacrifice to the Lord. Sanctify yourselves and come with me to the sacrifice." Then he consecrated Jesse and his sons and invited them to the sacrifice.

---

[2] You can read about these events in 1 Samuel 18, 19 to 20.

Now notice something. When Samuel took Jesse and his sons, David was not there. Samuel sanctified the brothers because he knew Jesse and he knew his boys. He didn't know there was a young one because they didn't invite David. They left him with the sheep. They didn't bring him around.

David is a little wild, a little strange. He has a bow that he flipped around and made a harp and he would sit on the side of the hill and play at night and sing to the glory of God. He would sing and the sheep would go *"Baaa."* He was always picking fights with something bigger than himself. He killed a bear, he killed a lion, then he ended up killing a giant. See, we don't want those kinds of preachers. We don't want those kinds of Equippers. We want the ones that hide in the trenches.

When David is going to fight Goliath, his brothers come and say, "What are you doing here? Go back home. You ain't got no business here."

What did David say? "I'm bringing you some bread and some wine."

They say, "Ok, that good. We got it, go back home, get out of here because we're going to hide and if you come, we will have to get out of hiding."

When the Leaders Seek the Lord, the People Get It Right

Sometimes people are Disqualified when they could have been Removed for a time. Know them that labor amongst you.

> *". . . he who turns a sinner from the error of his way will save a soul from death and cover a multitude of sins."—James 5:20*

When you're hiring and working with people, training and equipping them to be pastors and leaders, you have to see what the Holy Spirit sees. You have to hear what the Holy Spirit says. When you get it right, the people will get it right.

Seek the Lord. Seek His face. Find out what the Holy Spirit is saying.

"He who has an ear, let him hear what the Spirit says to the churches."—Revelation 2:7

22. Those Who Fill the Universe with Christ

"And the same one who descended is the one who ascended higher than all the heavens, so that he might fill the entire universe with himself."—Ephesians 4:10 NLT

We must become addicted Equippers. I used be a pusher of drugs but now I'm a people pusher. For the last 40 years I've been pushing people up the mountain.

Addicted to the Ministry of the Saints

"I urge you, brethren—you know the household of Stephanas, that it is the firstfruits of Achaia, and that they have devoted themselves to the ministry of the saints."—1 Corinthians 16:15

Paul said that *"they have devoted themselves to the ministry of the saints."* The word "devoted" is not in the original Greek. The original Greek word is "addicted." It is the same word used for being addicted to drugs. Those ministering to the saints are so devoted that it is like being addicted to others' success. They want you to become all that you're supposed to be in God.

I have been seeking God for 50 years. I am after God. I'm on the hunt. I'm searching every day for more of God and God keeps blessing me.

The other day I told someone, "I am a people mechanic." He responded, "I love it! I'm going to steal it."

Equippers are people mechanics who develop Christians in the churches who are destined to rebuild old ruins in every nation. Isaiah said that those from among us will rebuild waste places. They will make desolate cities new again.

"Those from among you
Shall build the old waste places;
You shall raise up the foundations of many
generations;
And you shall be called the Repairer of the Breach,
The Restorer of Streets to Dwell In."—Isaiah 58:12

"And they shall rebuild the old ruins,
They shall raise up the former desolations,
And they shall repair the ruined cities,
The desolations of many generations."—Isaiah 61:4

God's Focus Is the Church

"And I say also unto thee, That thou art Peter, and upon this
rock I will build my church; and the gates of hell shall not
prevail against it."—Matthew 16:18 KJV

Jesus declared that the sovereign work of God would be accomplished through the organism called the local church. He said, "I will build my church, and the gates of hell shall not prevail against it."

The Holy Spirit is bringing the universal church back to God's intended pattern—to cover the earth with the knowledge of His glory and to disciple nations (Matthew 28:19 -20). In the church, God raises up pastors and the fivefold ministry to be Equippers of those to be Sent to change nations.

The local church is the training center and distribution center where God's people become submitted to the Lord Jesus Christ and to the Holy Spirit and respond to His call to rebuild ruins. Then there can be ascending responsibility levels. There can be a sending of ministries and planting churches.

God's focus is the church. God is calling us to equip the next generation of preachers, the next generation of marketplace ministers, the next generation—in the church!

"And I also say to you that you are Peter, and on this rock I will build My church, and the gates of Hades shall not prevail against it."—Matthew 16:18

"And if he refuses to hear them, tell it to the church. But if he refuses even to hear the church, let him be to you like a heathen and a tax collector."
—Matthew 18:17

"But now I have written to you not to keep company with anyone named a brother, who is sexually immoral, or covetous, or an idolater, or a reviler, or a drunkard, or an extortioner—not even to eat with such a person.

"For what have I to do with judging those also who are outside? Do you not judge those who are inside? But those who are outside God judges. Therefore 'put away from yourselves the evil person.'"
—1 Corinthians 5:11-13

"Dare any of you, having a matter against another, go to law before the unrighteous, and not before the saints?"—1 Corinthians 6:1

"Now, therefore, you are no longer strangers and foreigners, but fellow citizens with the saints and members of the household of God."—Ephesians 2:19

"Therefore, as we have opportunity, let us do good to all, especially to those who are of the household of faith."—Galatians 6:10

"I, Jesus, have sent My angel to testify to you these things in the churches. I am the Root and the Offspring of David, the Bright and Morning Star."
—Revelation 22:16

"He who has an ear, let him hear what the Spirit says to the churches. To him who overcomes I will give to eat from the tree of life, which is in the midst of the Paradise of God."—Revelation 2:7

Getting Ready to Welcome the King of Glory

". . . that you put off, concerning your former conduct, the old man which grows corrupt according to the deceitful lusts, and be renewed in the spirit of your mind, and that you put on the new man which was created according to God, in true righteousness and holiness."—Ephesians 4:22-24

I'm out to see that there is a church that remains during this period of time until Jesus comes back. I believe there's a remnant church that's going to be without spot or wrinkle that will welcome the King of Glory when He comes back, and I want to be a part of that. And if I'm not alive, I want to make sure I pushed enough others over the edge that they're going to be a part of that.

"Repent therefore and be converted, that your sins may be blotted out, so that times of refreshing may come from the presence of the Lord, and that He may send Jesus Christ, who was preached to you before, whom heaven must receive until the times of restoration of all things"—Acts 3:19-21

MORE BOOKS BY BISHOP BART PIERCE

Seeking Our Brothers is the story of a body of believers reaching a city by reaching the needy through selfless acts of kindness that demonstrate the love of Jesus for humanity. The Kingdom of God can be established through the lives of believers to affect, and ultimately transform, every party of society. We must become, in reality, our brothers' keepers.

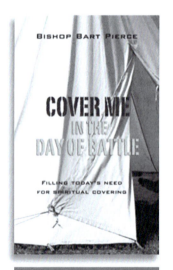

Life is full of daily battles. Why do good Christian soldiers-pastors, leaders, intercessors, and others-lose some of those battles? Is it possible that they fail to reach their greatest potential because they go to battle without the covering of a spiritual father?

In this day of do-it-yourselfism, Bishop Bart Pierce says it's time to address our need for fathers-both spiritual and natural. It's God's desire and the groan of the world for mature sons to come forth

Fathers, arise now, and raise up sons. Sons, arise and get your heads covered, and lets go to battle under the covering of God and our fathers. Then the curse of fatherlessness will be broken, and sons will turn to fathers and fathers will turn to sons, so that the Church can be the force God created it to be.

In this masterful book, Bart Pierce exposes the greatest scandal in history. He chronicles the radical plot of supernatural forces to silence the voices of truth. Over two millennia ago, a Roman soldier and "The Bribe of Great Price" spawned the greatest cover up in history. The Bribe quietly survived the rise and fall of dictators, parliaments, Kingdoms, Empires and Nations. In a post-modern era, it openly employs the sciences, political systems, religion and mass media. Due to an elaborate deception, even the Church has aided in this conspiracy. This book is definitely a page-turner for every believer, seeker and conspiracy theorist alike. It is an unforgettable journey!

In the book The 5-G Shift, Bishop Bart Pierce challenges generations that have grown up in a "what's in it for me" culture to look outside themselves to mentor and make a difference in the next generation. If we do not change the current tide of selfishness to selflessness, the church and hope for the church in America is dwindling away until church buildings will only be empty sepulchers of where God used to be. Now is the time to awaken believers to mentor and care about the next generation.